EQUIP™ Leadership Series

CONTAGIOUS
LEADERSHIP
WORKBOOK

JOHN C. MAXWELL AND EQUIP™

THOMAS NELSON
Since 1798

NASHVILLE   DALLAS   MEXICO CITY   RIO DE JANEIRO   BEIJING

Published by Nelson Impact, a Division of Thomas Nelson, Inc., P.O. Box 141000,
Nashville, Tennessee, 37214.

Published in association with Yates & Yates, LLP, Attorneys and Counselors,
Orange, California.

Scripture references are from the following sources:

The Holy Bible, New International Version (NIV). Copyright © 1973, 1978,
1984. International Bible Society. Used by permission of Zondervan Bible
Publishers.

The New King James Version (NKJV), copyright © 1982 by Thomas Nelson, Inc.
Used by permission. All rights reserved.

The Holy Bible, New Living Translation (NLT), copyright © 1996. Used by
permission of Tyndale House Publishers, Inc. Wheaton, IL 60189. All rights
reserved.

New American Standard Bible (NASB). Copyright © 1960, 1962, 1963, 1968,
1971, 1972, 1973, 1975, 1977, 1995 by The Lockman Foundation. Used by
permission.

ISBN-10: 1-4185-1784-4

ISBN-13: 978-141851-784-7

06 07 08 09 VIC 9 8 7 6 5 4 3 2 1

Introduction

by Dr. John C. Maxwell

Leadership lifts people. Leadership lifts people from the life they have to the life they *could* have. I have long believed this even as a young boy growing up, as I watched my dad model leadership in our home, in the pastorate, and as a college president.

Over the past thirty-plus years, I have practiced leadership firsthand while growing churches and building companies. Now, my greatest joy comes from training others in leadership. And that's why I want to make this leadership training material available to you.

Until now, this leadership training material has only been available in my international endeavors. In 1996, I partnered with a group of trusted friends to launch EQUIP, a non-profit ministry dedicated to equipping Christians worldwide with the leadership skills needed for advancing the Great Commission in their communities, workplaces, and churches. Under the leadership of current President and CEO John Hull, our leadership training has been translated into thirty-five languages and has been taught in more than one hundred countries around the world. By March 1, 2006, EQUIP realized a personal dream of mine by training *one million* international leaders! And the ministry continues to grow, with a goal to train and equip an additional five million leaders on five continents over the next five years.

The purpose of the Great Commission is to reach people who are far from God and to raise them up to be fully devoted followers of Jesus Christ. But honestly, this goal is not possible

The Great Commission

Then Jesus came to them and said, "All authority in heaven and on earth has been given to me. Therefore go and make disciples of all nations, baptizing them in the name of the Father and of the Son and of the Holy Spirit, and teaching them to obey everything I have commanded you. And surely I am with you always, to the very end of the age."

— Matt. 28:18-20 NIV

without God-anointed spiritual leadership. Thousands of pastors love God, pray faithfully, work hard, and possess deep love and compassion for people—but their churches experience little or no growth. They need training and inspiration to get the mission accomplished.

It is our heart's desire that you and your church succeed in your passion to reach people for Christ, and I want to help you do this by teaching you how to train leaders in your church.

This material is perfect for you if . . .

- you want to develop your people by investing in them personally.

- you want to grow your church.

- you are busy and have little time to write your own leadership training curriculum.

- you want high-quality, proven, field-tested material developed by veteran leaders.

- you want to equip your leaders to excel in their ministries.

How to Use This Material

This leadership kit, *Contagious Leadership*, features two separate tracks of study:

1. The first track is for the Pastor, Facilitator, or anyone else who will be teaching this material. In this track of study, you should work through *Contagious Leadership Workbook* in its entirety. The comprehensive material in this workbook corresponds directly with the *Contagious Leadership* Audio CD found in this kit. Before teaching the workbook lesson to others, listen to each audio lesson

on CD. Each of the twelve lessons addresses Christian leadership in one of the three major facets of leadership development — spiritual formation, skill formation, and strategic formation.

2. This kit also includes a complete line of study crafted specifically for small group use. The *Contagious Leadership Small Group Study Lessons* can be found on the DVD, which corresponds directly with the *Small Group Study Guide* found on the CD-ROM. Each of the twelve DVD lessons is about twenty minutes long. As you lead your small group, watch the DVD lesson first as a group, and then go through the Small Group Study questions together for discussion, assessment, and application. The *Small Group Study Guide* is downloadable and reproducible for your convenience.

Where can I use this material?

This material is perfect for:

- **Key leader groups**

  Key leader groups refer to groups such as the church staff, the local church board, Sunday school teachers, or any other groups essential to your ministry.

- **Teaching venues**

  A teaching venue refers to any number of possible classroom environments. From Sunday and Wednesday night classes, to a special seminar on a weekend, to a standard Sunday school class, you could offer this material as an elective course to a broad number of people.

- **Outreach opportunities**

  This opportunity is exciting. You could open up this leadership training to business people in your community. Encourage the business leaders in your church to invite their colleagues to attend, and adapt to make a percentage of your illustrations about the home and marketplace, rather than about church situations only.

- **Small groups**

  Small group leaders are always looking for quality material to share in their groups. What better way to lift people up than to teach them about leadership? The twelve-week study is perfect for this format.

- **Christian schools**

  There is growing enthusiasm to get leadership training to young Christians. We are seeing that high schools are interested in teaching leadership to their students.

The above applications can be used in a number of ways or processes and be very effective. Remember, do what works best for your group. I recommend that if you have not done much leadership training in the past, or have not been consistent, that you start small and slow and build the process over the course of time. Don't get too hung up in the details of training people in a certain way, as there is no "one way." Put your energy and effort into fully engaging your heart and delivering a world-class experience for those going through the material.

There are several different timelines you can use as you go through the material:

- **Weekly sessions for twelve weeks**

  This is the most obvious but not the only method. Simply select twelve weeks that work best for you, usually in the Spring or Fall.

- **Monthly sessions for one year or twice a month for six months**

  This is a slow pace, but the advantage is that you can gain great depth and follow-up on many of the concepts explored by going slowly through the material. This method is good for implementing what you learn through practice and application.

- **Two Saturday seminars**

  By teaching six lessons at a time, you can train your leaders in a more intensive "fast track" system.

- **A weekend retreat setting**

  Similar to the Saturday seminars, you can take a weekend away and press through the material in a variety of small group and teaching applications.

- **A special summer course**

  Why should summer be a "down time"? Why not offer an impacting course over four Wednesday nights, covering three lessons a night? Your group could meet in someone's home and gather over a potluck dinner.

Again, there are so many possibilities for applying this material to your needs. The sky is the limit!

Three Keys

As you are working through this material in preparation to teach others, remember to:

1. Keep it simple.

Often, there is a tendency to overcomplicate leadership training. Keep it simple. The only wrong way to do it is not to do it at all. In this leadership training, simply listen to the lesson, learn and practice yourself, and teach it to your leaders and aspiring leaders.

2. Stay consistent.

Over-complication leads to breakdown in consistency. If you make it too difficult or cumbersome, you will get frustrated and want to quit. Stay in the game. Think long term. You are working to develop a life practice, not a just a program.

3. Expect results.

This is a key point. Know why you are developing leaders, what they should "look like" (skills, abilities, qualities, and characteristics), and turn them loose— not into busy work, but into kingdom efforts that will make a difference. Expect much and you will receive much.

Getting Started

- Know why you want to develop leaders in your church or organization.

- Pray for God's favor throughout the process.

- Get buy-in from the top 5 percent of your leaders.

- Decide which timeline you'd like to use for studying the material.

- Organize your dates, times, and places.

- Review and become very familiar with the material.

- Give the leaders or teachers who will do the training adequate time to prepare.

- Cast a vision for the process and recruit the people you want to participate.

- Get started!

Keep in mind that leadership is best learned in a leadership culture. That means that you yourself must also keep growing as a leader, casting vision for the value of leadership and providing ongoing training.

Remember, hundreds of thousands of people have used this material around the world. It has worked for them—it can work for you!

Table of Contents

God's Call for Us to Lead

Lesson 1
Why and How God Calls Us to Lead

BIBLICAL
BASIS

Let us make man in our image…
and let him rule. (Gen. 1:26 NIV)

Christians have debated the subject of leadership for centuries. *Is it biblical to lead? Are we not called to be followers instead of leaders? Are we not called to be servants instead of rulers? Can we honestly believe that leadership is a biblical idea?*

When we study the Bible closely, we see that leadership is, indeed, God's idea. God is not only the Ultimate Leader, but He has called us to lead as well.

Born to Lead

Consider this. The first description of mankind in the Bible involves leadership. God designed us to lead, to have authority and take dominion. According to Genesis 1:26–31, you and I were born to lead. Study this Scripture . . .

> *Then God said, "Let us make man in our image, in our likeness, and let them rule over the fish of the sea, and the birds of the air, over the livestock, over all the earth, and over all the creatures that move along the ground." (Gen. 1:26 NIV)*

1. **Being made in God's image means we were created to LEAD.**

According to verse 26, we are made in God's image. What does this mean? One clue is found in the next phrase: "and

13

Contagious Leadership Workbook

let them rule." Knowing we were fashioned to lead and rule is part of what it means to be like God.

2. God gave humans AUTHORITY over the whole earth.

We should be comfortable with two positions. The first position is being under God's authority. The second position is being in authority over the world. God has given us this calling. We must discover what it means to lead like God does.

3. If God told us to rule, we must have the ABILITY to do it.

God never commands us to do anything without enabling us to do it. You and I have the ability to lead because God created us and commanded us to do so. Based on your gifts and personality, you have the ability to lead in some area.

EXAMINE THE WORD

Being Salt and Light

In the New Testament, God confirms this calling to influence others. Look at Matthew 5:13–16 NASB:

You are the salt of the earth; but if the salt has become tasteless, how will it be made salty again? . . . You are the light of the world. A city set on a hill cannot be hidden. Nor do men light a lamp, and put it under the peck-measure, but on the lampstand; and it gives light to all who are in the house. Let your light shine before men in such a way that they may see your good works, and glorify your Father who is in heaven.

Salt influences the food we eat. Light influences the homes in which we live. Jesus is calling us to embrace our calling to influence and to shine wherever we go. The Apostle Paul took this calling seriously when he said:

14

Therefore knowing the fear of the Lord, we persuade men . . .
(2 Cor. 5:11 NASB)

Divine Permission to Lead

Many of us feel like Moses did when he faced God at
the burning bush, in Exodus 3–4. He felt inadequate and
unprepared to lead. But that's what God called him to do.
Many potential leaders in the Bible were afraid and ran from
their call. God had to give them permission to lead.

Most of us can list why we don't lead effectively, just
as Moses did. When God called him, he instantly had five
excuses why he couldn't lead. Notice how God responds to
them.

Excuse One: Who am I? (Exod. 3:11)

Moses struggled with his identity. He just didn't feel qualified.
He thought God picked the wrong leader. God's response: *It
doesn't matter who you are. I've called you. I am with you.*

Excuse Two: Who are you? (Exod. 3:13)

Moses struggled with intimacy. He didn't know God well
enough to describe Him to the people. His relationship
with God was weak. God's response: *I AM WHO I AM. I'm
everything you need.*

Excuse Three: What if they don't listen? (Exod. 4:1)

Moses struggled with intimidation. He worried about people's
reaction to him. God's response: *When I am finished, they'll
listen. Trust me.*

15

Excuse Four: I've never been a good speaker. (Exod. 4:10)

Moses struggled with inadequacy. Who would follow him if he couldn't speak well? God's response: *Guess who made your mouth? I'm the source of your gifts.*

Excuse Five: I know you can find someone else. (Exod. 4:13)

Moses struggled with inferiority. He compared himself with other more competent people, and he felt weak. God's response: *Okay, I will let Aaron go with you . . . but I'm still calling you.*

Question: What excuses do you have for not leading well? What do you believe God's response might be?

_____

_____

_____

_____

_____

Leadership Is Influence

J. Oswald Sanders said it first: Leadership is influence. Nothing more. Nothing less. It is about influencing others in a worthwhile cause. It is not dependent on titles or positions. It is dependent on someone catching a vision from God and mobilizing others to join them in its fulfillment. When this happens, leadership arises in its purest form. It happens to every organization at one point or another, especially when there's no system or plan. In those times, there is no expectation of progress. Today, many regions of the world are crying for godly, effective leaders. The leader must earn the right to lead and others *choose to follow*.

The Period of the Judges

Before Israel adopted a monarchy and Saul was appointed to be their king, they experienced an era of time called the period of the judges. It was a season when pure leadership was required. Every judge who led was a pioneer. The following verse appears more than once in the book of Judges:

> *In those days Israel had no king; everyone did as he saw fit.*
> (Judges 21:25 NIV)

Here are six reasons why this period was a leadership-intensive season:

1. Chaos reigned because there was no precedent for *authority* or *accountability*.

2. Since the Jews first occupied Canaan, aggressive *enemies* surrounded them.

17

3. There were no government *funds* for national defense or safety.

4. Other *nations* influenced Israel with their idols and superstitions.

5. Heroes like Moses and Joshua were *dead* and there was no *expectation* of order.

6. Momentum and morale were *low,* so growth was hard not easy.

Fourteen judges led Israel during this period. Each leader started his/her leadership role from scratch. These are the ones we know about: Othniel, Ehud, Shamgar, Deborah, Gideon, Abimelech, Tola, Jair, Jephthah, Ibzan, Elon, Abdon, Samson, and Samuel.

Certainly, we know more about some of these judges than others. However, from the text we can summarize how effective leaders led during Israel's most difficult season. During these times, leaders must go back to the basics. The basics are clear during this period in Israel's history. The judges had the following characteristics in common.

The Basics of Effective Leaders:

1. THEY PERCEIVE A NEED

Contrary to what many think about leadership today,
during this time leadership always began with a need.
In Judges, it didn't start when someone wanted to fill
an empty position. There were no positions to fill. There
was no protocol or structure at all. There was no vote
for deacons or Sunday school teachers. If you led it was
because you saw a need and got others to help you meet
it. The judges all got their start when they saw a specific
problem they could address.

KEY POINTS

- **Othniel:** Found Israel surrounded by Mesopotamia.
  He stepped forward to recruit and lead an army of
  Hebrews against the king. He prevailed. This led to
  forty years of peace.

- **Ehud:** Observed the Moabites dominating his
  people, and decided he'd had enough. He led Israel
  to a rousing victory over Moab. This led to eighty
  years of peace.

- **Shamgar:** Stepped forward when the Philistines had
  oppressed Israel for years. When he personally struck
  down six hundred soldiers, he inspired his army to
  victory.

When Leadership Is Pure . . .

a. It always starts with a need.

b. That need sparks passion within a person.

c. That person acts in response to the need.

d. This action moves others to cooperate.

APPLICATION: When you hear the many needs around you, which one strikes a chord within your heart? What kind of "specialist" are you called to become? What will you do before you die? What will be your significant contribution?

_____

_____

_____

2. THEY POSSESS A GIFT

In each case in Judges, the leaders emerged because they had an obvious gift. They possessed some ability that fit the need of the moment perfectly. They were competent in a relevant arena. Their gift solved a problem. In each case, the "gift" was from God but took on different forms. It was:

a. **A spiritual gift:** Samson had a spiritual gift connected to his Nazarite vow.

b. **A natural talent:** Deborah had a natural talent for strategy and wisdom.

c. **An acquired skill:** Gideon and Jephthah developed their skills to lead over time.

God has put something inside each of us that is to be delivered to the people around us. In other words, everyone has something we all need. When we find it, we naturally influence others.

When Leadership Is Pure . . .

a. A person finds a GIFT inside of them.

b. They groom and DEVELOP that gift.

c. They eventually match that gift with a place of SERVICE.

d. The gift provides a platform for INFLUENCE.

e. They eventually flourish because of their GIFT.

We naturally lead in the areas of our gifts. In our gift areas, we are most . . .

* Intuitive   * Satisfied

* Productive   * Natural

* Comfortable   * Influential

APPLICATION: How about you? What is your primary gift? What contribution do you make to the body of Christ that would be most missed if you were gone? What do you add to your organization that you do best?

_____

_____

_____

3. THEY PARADE A PASSION

When an outward need and an inward gift match, the leader often follows by becoming consumed with a passion. This passion is compelling to others; the leader can't help but share it with those who want to get involved. In the book of Judges, several leaders experienced this kind of inward chemistry that sparks passion. Here are the ingredients for passion:

Passion comes when a leader has complementary . . .

  a. **BURDENS**: Your interests and concerns

  b. **CONVICTIONS**: Your values, principles, and beliefs

  c. **GIFTS**: Your God-given abilities

  d. **NEEDS**: Your desperate circumstances

  e. **OPPORTUNITIES**: Your occasion to get involved

Passion makes up for a lack of resources. No doubt, resources are nice to have, but many of the Judges were not rich in money, people, or talent when they started. Gideon was scared. Samson lacked a moral backbone. Jephthah was impetuous. Abimelech got over-zealous and had to be reprimanded. It appears that Ibzan, Elon, and Abdon might have been elderly. This doesn't stop people if they have passion.

APPLICATION: Passion generally begins with interests. What are your interests as they relate to leadership and the needs around you? What makes you cry or makes you angry? What do you feel so strongly about that you are driven to act?

4. THEY PERSUADE A PEOPLE

True leaders eventually come to the point where they attract and empower others to their passion. Sometimes they just find others who share the same passion. One thing is sure, genuine leaders connect with others. This is what separates an entrepreneur and a leader. Leaders don't act alone. They have followers. They have to, because they have a cause that's bigger than they are. They need others to pull it off.

- **Gideon:** Gideon was told to gather an army and attack the Midianites. He recruited too many men, and God had to trim the size of his army or Gideon might take credit for the win! This leader persuaded too many people to follow! If only we had the same problem.

- **Deborah:** Although she was a woman, Israel was fully persuaded by Deborah. Whatever she determined to do, the people followed. Barak even insisted she go with him to battle. He understood who had influence.

- **Samuel:** The strongest of all the Judges, Samuel was the most influential leader between the time of Moses and David. His leadership spanned two generations. Both old and young listened to him. Even kings looked up to him. He anointed both Saul and David as kings. He was a leader of leaders.

Proven practices for getting things done . . .

a. What gets talked about gets done.

b. What gets trained for gets done.

c. What gets measured gets done.

d. What gets budgeted gets done.

e. What gets confronted gets done.

f. What gets rewarded gets done.

APPLICATION: How about you? Who has bought into your leadership 100 percent? Whom do you persuade? Is it the old or the young? Are they leaders or followers? How do you persuade people to take the journey with you? When do you influence others? Where do you influence them?

5. THEY PURSUE A PURPOSE

A final observation is that every judge could lead because he/she followed a distinct purpose laid out before him/her. They moved in a direction to reach a specific goal. No judge desired only to maintain status quo. Each felt he/she had a divine assignment to perform. You might call it his/her life purpose. It became a consuming accountability partner.

It would be difficult to separate leadership from purpose. I cannot imagine leading without a clear sense of a God-given purpose. Perhaps this is why so many churches fail to bear fruit. There is no clear, defined, agreed-upon mission.

In Judges, Their Purpose Was . . .

a. **Personal:** It fit their gifts and passions.

b. **Measurable:** It involved activity that could be evaluated.

c. **Memorable:** It was specific enough to be remembered and embraced.

d. **Meaningful:** It surrounded national issues that made a difference.

e. **Mobile:** It could travel with them wherever they found themselves.

f. **Moral:** It was right. They not only felt it could be done but should be done.

• **Deborah:** Her sole purpose was to liberate Israel from the Caananites. She laid out a plan, provided the resources, commissioned Barak to lead the army, and when he refused to lead the attack alone, she went with him.

ASSESSMENT: Do you follow your purpose? How do you compare to the judges?

ACTION PLAN

_____

_____

_____

_____

APPLICATION: What is your clear purpose? Have you defined it? Do the key people in your organization agree upon what it is and how it should be pursued?

_____

_____

_____

_____

_____

Self-Evaluation:

In your own life, how well do you display the five characteristics demonstrated by leaders in the book of Judges?

1. Perceive a Need

1   2   3   4   5   6   7   8   9   10

2. Possess a Gift

1   2   3   4   5   6   7   8   9   10

3. Parade a Passion

1   2   3   4   5   6   7   8   9   10

4. Persuade a People

1   2   3   4   5   6   7   8   9   10

5. Pursue a Purpose

1   2   3   4   5   6   7   8   9   10

The Heart of a Leader

Lesson 2

Developing the Qualities that Set Leaders Apart from Others

So he shepherded them according to the integrity of his heart, And guided them with his skillful hands.
(Ps. 78:72 NASB)

In every age there comes a time when a leader must step forward to meet the needs of the hour. Therefore, there is no potential leader who does not have an opportunity to make a positive difference in society. Tragically, there are times when a leader does not rise to that hour.

Why is it that when circumstances call for it, a leader does not rise up? Many times, it is because people have not prepared their hearts to serve. So, what kind of hearts do we need?

Preparing Our Hearts

It is important that leaders develop their "skills" in order to lead effectively. First, however, there are several important qualities of the heart that every great leader should build into his or her life.

In Acts 9:3–6 NKJV Saul is traveling to Damascus when he meets Jesus face to face. His two questions are the right questions asked in the right order. First he asks, *Who are you, Lord?* Then he asks, *What would you have me to do?* These are questions that should guide a leader's life.

EXAMINE THE WORD

The Leader God Uses . . .

1. . . . has a great PURPOSE in life.

But what things were gain to me, these I have counted loss for Christ. Yet indeed I also count all things loss for the excellence of the knowledge of Christ Jesus my Lord, for whom I have suffered the loss of all things, and count them as rubbish, that I may gain Christ and be found in Him . . . that I may know Him and the power of His resurrection, and the fellowship of His sufferings, being conformed to His death, if, by any means, I may attain to the resurrection from the dead. (Phil. 3:7–11 NKJV)

Do you know your God-given purpose? You must answer these questions:

a. What are your burdens?

b. What are your spiritual gifts?

c. What are your natural talents?

d. What are your desires and passions?

e. What do others affirm about you?

f. What are your dreams and visions?

g. What opportunities are in front of you?

2. . . . has by God's grace, removed any HINDRANCE from his life.

Therefore we also, since we are surrounded by so great a cloud of witnesses, let us lay aside every weight, and the sin which so easily ensnares us, and let us run with endurance the race that is set before us, looking unto Jesus, the author and finisher of our faith, who for the joy that was set before Him endured the cross, despising the shame, and has sat down at the right hand of the throne of God. (Heb. 12:1–2 NKJV)

Character and integrity are indispensable. Character can be defined as self-leadership. Once you lead yourself well, others may want to follow. It is the foundation on which the leader's life is built. It all begins with character because leadership operates on the basis of trust. If people don't trust you, they won't follow you. Here is what character does for a leader:

a. Character communicates *credibility*.

b. Character harnesses *respect*.

c. Character creates *consistency*.

d. Character earns *trust*.

In order to build strong character, leaders must choose to:

a. Develop personal *discipline*.

b. Develop a personal *security* and *identity*.

c. Develop personal *convictions*, *values*, and *ethics*.

3. . . . has placed himself absolutely at God's DISPOSAL.

I beseech you therefore, brethren, by the mercies of God, that you present your bodies a living sacrifice, holy, acceptable to God, which is your reasonable service. And do not be conformed to this world, but be transformed by the renewing of your mind, that you may prove what is that good and acceptable and perfect will of God. (Rom. 12:1–2 NKJV)

31

To lead others, we must develop three attitudes of total surrender to God:

   a. We must have nothing to *prove*. (We don't try to project our self worth.)

   b. We must have nothing to *lose*. (We don't strive for image or popularity.)

   c. We must have nothing to *hide*. (We don't play games but are transparent.)

4. . . . has learned how to prevail in PRAYER.

Is anyone among you suffering? Let him pray . . . Is anyone among you sick? Let him call for the elders of the church, and let them pray over him . . . And the prayer of faith will save the sick, and the Lord will raise him up . . . Confess your trespasses to one another, and pray for one another, that you may be healed. The effective, fervent prayer of a righteous man avails much. (James 5:13–17 NKJV)

Jesus listed three kinds of prayer (Matt. 7:7) in which leaders must learn to prevail:

   a. **Ask:** This is the prayer of faith. With it we lay hold of God's promises by faith.

   b. **Seek:** This is the prayer of dedication. With it we seek to know God's will.

   c. **Knock:** This is the prayer of intercession. With it we pray for someone who cannot or will not pray for themselves.

5. . . . is a student of GOD'S WORD.

All Scripture is given by inspiration of God, and is profitable for doctrine, for reproof, for correction, for instruction in righteousness, that the man of God may be complete, thoroughly equipped for every good work. (2 Tim. 3:16–17 NKJV)

Do your best to present yourself to God as one approved, a workman who does not need to be ashamed and who correctly handles the word of truth. (2 Tim. 2:15 NIV)

Students of God's Word examine Scripture to understand its meaning for . . .

  a. **One Time:** What did it mean at one time, to the original audience?

  b. **All Time:** What is the universal and timeless principle we can learn?

  c. **Now Time:** What should we presently do in response to it?

6. . . . has a vital, life-changing MESSAGE for a lost world.

Holding fast the word of life, so that in the day of Christ I will have reason to glory because I did not run in vain nor toil in vain. (Phil. 2:16 NASB)

In Romans 1:14–16, the Apostle Paul expressed three attitudes concerning the Gospel:

  a. **I am *obligated*** (v. 14): Sharing the message is a debt I owe to the world.

  b. **I am *eager*** (v. 15): I am on fire to share this message with the world.

Contagious Leadership Workbook

c. **I am *not ashamed*** (v. 16): I will share it because it alone can save us.

7. . . . has a FAITH that expects result.

And not being weak in faith, he did not consider his own body, already dead . . . and the deadness of Sarah's womb. He did not waver at the promise of God through unbelief, but was strengthened in faith, giving glory to God, and being fully convinced that what He had promised He was also able to perform. (Rom. 4:19–21 NKJV)

Hebrews describes men and women of faith and what they each had in common:

a. **Vision:** Each of them "saw" the promises from far off.

b. **Confidence:** Each of them were assured of the promises of God.

c. **Hunger:** Each of them embraced and owned the promises as their own.

d. **Resolve:** They confessed that they were pilgrims on the earth.

e. **Dreams:** Their God-given dreams, not their memories, consumed them.

8. . . . chooses to SERVE in attitude and action.

In Philippians 2:5–11, Paul writes about how we should embrace the same "mind" that drove Jesus to lead by serving in attitude and action:

Who, being in the form of God, did not consider it robbery to be equal with God, but made Himself of no reputation, taking the form of a bondservant, and coming in the likeness of men.

And being found in appearance as a man, He humbled Himself and became obedient to the point of death, even the death of the cross. (Phil. 2:6–8 NKJV)

Although He was God, He did not cling to His position, but rather to His purpose. He was not position-conscious, but purpose-conscious. He knew the best way to accomplish His purpose was to serve people. A leader naturally arises when someone determines to serve.

It always starts with a need:

a. That need sparks passion within a person.

b. That person acts in response to the need.

c. This action moves others to cooperate.

9. . . . stirs up the GIFTS in themselves and others.

Till I come, give attention to reading, to exhortation, to doctrine. Do not neglect the gift that is in you, which was given to you by prophecy with the laying on of the hands of the eldership. Meditate on these things; give yourself entirely to them, that your progress may be evident to all. Take heed to yourself and to the doctrine. Continue in them, for in doing this you will save both yourself and those who hear you. (1 Tim. 4:13–16 NKJV)

Leaders naturally arise when they find their gifts and use them to serve. It usually follows this order:

a. First, a leader identifies a primary gift.

b. Second, he/she develops that gift.

c. Third, he/she matches that gift with a place of service.

d. Fourth, that gift provides a platform for influence.

35

e. Finally, the leader eventually flourishes because of his/her gift.

10. . . . is SECURE enough to empower others.

Jesus, knowing that the Father had given all things into His hands, and that He had come forth from God and was going back to God, got up from supper, and laid aside His garments; and taking a towel, He girded Himself. Then He poured water into the basin, and began to wash the disciples' feet . . . " (John 13:3–5 NASB)

In John 13, Jesus modeled a servant's heart when He washed the disciples' feet. Note what enabled Him to do this: a strong sense of security in His identity. Leaders who are not secure in their identity in Christ will eventually sabotage their leadership. Insecure leaders become their own worst enemy. They cannot share victories or sorrows. The Law of Empowerment reminds us: Only secure leaders give their power to others. Here is the difference between secure leaders and insecure leaders:

SECURE LEADERS	INSECURE LEADERS
a. The secure focus on towels.	a. The insecure focus on titles.
b. The secure draw strength from identity.	b. The insecure draw strength from image.
c. The secure pursue service to others.	c. The insecure pursue status with others.
d. The secure want to add value to others.	d. The insecure want to gain value from others.

11. . . . lives under the ANOINTING of the Holy Spirit.

And do not be drunk with wine, in which is dissipation; but be filled with the Spirit, speaking to one another in psalms and hymns and spiritual songs, singing and making melody in your heart to the Lord, giving thanks always for all things to God the Father in the name of our Lord Jesus Christ. (Eph. 5:18–20 NKJV)

a. Anointed leaders possess spiritual authority over others.

b. Anointed leaders consistently see God move in their ministries.

c. Anointed leaders' lives demand a supernatural explanation.

12. . . . has chosen to be an EXAMPLE before he leads others.

Do you not know that those who run in a race all run, but one receives the prize? Run in such a way that you may obtain it. And everyone who competes for the prize is temperate in all things. Now they do it to obtain a perishable crown, but we for an imperishable crown. Therefore, I run thus: not with uncertainty. Thus I fight: not as one who beats the air. But I discipline my body and bring it into subjection, lest, when I have preached to others, I myself should become disqualified. (1 Cor. 9:24–27 NKJV)

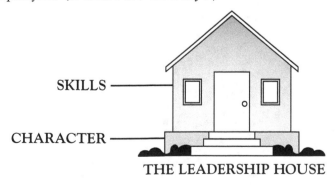

SKILLS

CHARACTER

THE LEADERSHIP HOUSE

TRUTH IN A PICTURE

Reasons why a heart of integrity is so important to leaders:

- Leadership functions on the basis of *trust*.

- Integrity has high influence *value*.

- Our tendency is to work harder on our *image* than on our integrity.

- Integrity means *living* the truth myself, before leading others.

- A charismatic personality may draw people, but only *integrity* will keep them.

- Integrity is a *victory*, not a gift.

- You will only *become* what you are becoming — right now.

- Leaders are to live by a higher *standard* than followers.

ASSESSMENT: If you were to evaluate yourself, how do you feel you would rank in the area of character? How is your leader's heart?

ACTION PLAN

_____

_____

_____

_____

APPLICATION: What are some activities and/or disciplines you could apply in your life in order to develop a stronger character?

I Have a Dream!

Lesson 3

Capturing and Implementing a God-Given Vision

All these people were still living by faith when they died. They did not receive the things promised; they only saw them and welcomed them from a distance.
(Heb. 11:13a NIV)

WHAT IS VISION?

It would be difficult to separate leadership from vision. All good leaders are driven by vision. They are not satisfied with simply maintaining the status quo. They long to take their ministry somewhere. But just what is *vision?* Some have attempted to define it below . . .

- "Vision is seeing the future, in the present, built on the past."

- "Vision is seeing the invisible and making it visible."

- "Vision is an informed bridge from the present to a better future."

For our purposes, let me suggest the following definition for you to consider. Vision is:

41

A CLEAR MENTAL PICTURE OF A BETTER
TOMORROW, GIVEN BY GOD, WHICH MOVES A
PERSON TO BELIEVE THAT IT NOT ONLY COULD BE
DONE, BUT IT SHOULD BE DONE.

Robert Greenleaf, in his book *The Servant as Leader*, says,
"Foresight is the 'lead' that the leader has. Once he loses this
lead and events start to force him to act, he is a leader in name
only. He is not leading; he is reacting to immediate events and
he probably will not remain the leader." People long for leaders
to give them hope — a picture of where they should go.

    Vision is a picture held in your mind's eye of the way
things could or should be in the days ahead. It is an internal
and personal portrait of a preferred future. Eventually, you will
have to paint this mental picture inside others if you wish the
vision to materialize in your ministry. Just as God has used your
imagination to create this view of the future, you will have to
help others catch the same vision inside of them — so that
they can share in its implementation.

Note the ingredients of a divine vision:

1. **A clear picture:** It serves as a sort of map on the inside.

2. **A positive change:** It improves present conditions by
   introducing God's kingdom.

3. **A future focus:** It furnishes direction to the unseen
   future.

4. **A gift from God:** It is divinely inspired, not humanly
   manipulated.

5. **A chosen people and time:** It is for a select leader and
   group at a given time.

Question: Have you ever been a part of catching and implementing a vision?

KEY
POINTS

The Birth of a Vision

For many leaders, their visions begin as ideas, without much detail or clarity. As time passes, the ideas turn into major areas of interest and soon become a passion. They take shape and form inside their minds and hearts. In many ways, the birth of a *vision* is much like the birth of a *child*. They go through various stages as they mature. Notice these stages below.

1. INTIMACY

In the same way that a husband and wife must join together to give birth to a son or daughter, a leader must experience intimacy with God in order to conceive a vision. People who catch a vision from God have spent time with Him in worship, quietness, solitude, and reflection. This union provides God the opportunity to speak and to reveal what He wants the leader to do. He plants the vision-seed inside you.

2. CONCEPTION

God may not communicate a vision every time you meet with Him. Conception doesn't occur every time a husband and wife come together. However, when God does reveal a vision to you, it comes in seed form and must grow inside of you. He plants the vision in you, and in the beginning

43

it may still seem unclear, not fully formed. Remember this: God is the husband, you are the bride of Christ. Just as a baby looks like both mom and dad, as the vision grows, it will look like God (it will center around His priorities) and it will look like you (it will match your interests and gifts).

3. GESTATION

This is the longest period of time in the process. It takes nine months for a child to be born. A vision from God may take even longer. During this time, the leader identifies with the problem, intercedes for the people, and intervenes in the process. The vision is forming inside the leader. When a baby is forming inside his mother, it changes the mother dramatically. So it is with a vision. God's vision will stretch you, and you will never be satisfied again with a man-made idea.

4. LABOR

This stage is often the most painful. Just prior to the birth of a vision, the labor becomes hard. Similar to the birth of a child, the labor pains become more frequent and more intense. This is a sign the birth is near. So it is with a God-given vision. The Enemy often comes to steal the vision just before it comes to pass — bringing pain and struggle. The fight intensifies. He wants us to abort the vision. Don't give up. Labor is a good sign that something is about to happen!

5. BIRTH

Finally, the vision is born. All that has been occurring inside the leader is ultimately realized. Everyone can see the fruit of the prayer, planning, and work. In fact, often many come to celebrate with you at this point, and you may wonder where they were when you were struggling to keep the vision alive! Don't get angry. Let them celebrate with you, and invite them to help you parent the vision. The vision must now grow up and eventually stand on its own.

Question: What stage are you experiencing now?

_____

_____

_____

Man-Made Vision	God-Given Vision
a. You create it based on your gifts and skills.	a. You receive it as a revelation from God.
b. Its fulfillment rests on staying ahead of others.	b. Its fulfillment rests on the leader's obedience.
c. Other similar organizations are seen as competitors.	c. Other similar ministries are seen as complementary.
d. Its goal is to build your organization and generate revenue.	d. Its goal is to serve people, advance God's rule, and to honor God.

Contagious Leadership Workbook

ULTIMATE VISION

THE LEADER

PROCESS

Steps to Fulfilling God's Vision
Matthew 9:35–10:8 NIV

Matthew 9:35–10:8 mark a pivotal point in Jesus's ministry. Until this point, Jesus was doing the ministry while the disciples watched. Read this passage and observe the process and strategy Jesus adopts as He fulfills His God-given vision. Christ models some steps for us to take today.

1. Get active in SERVICE and initiate obedience.

Jesus went through all the towns and villages (9:35a).

Jesus did not sit around by the Sea of Galilee waiting for ministry opportunities to come to Him. He was out, talking to people, entering their lives. He actively served people where they were. We must remember God usually shares His vision with those who are obeying what they already know to do.

2. Communicate the REVELATION you have already.

Teaching in their synagogues, preaching the good news of the kingdom (9:35b).

Do you realize that you already know 95 percent of God's will? "How?" you may ask. Open your Bible. God revealed 95 percent of His will for our lives there, yet we constantly badger Him for the other 5 percent: questions like who will be our mate, what career we will have, or what is our future? God simply says: Obey what you already know, and then I will show you more.

3. OBSERVE and understand the reality of human conditions.

When He saw the crowds (9:36a).

Jesus was there among the people watching them. He saw the pained expressions on their faces and the physical ailments that afflicted them as they came to Him for healing. He stopped long enough to observe and understand their condition.

4. Allow God to BURDEN you with a specific need.

He had compassion on them, because they were harassed and helpless, like sheep without a shepherd (9:36b).

Jesus's heart was moved. He felt pity for them and the condition they were in. This is how every vision begins: with a burden. You see something wrong, something that is not being done that should be done. From this a vision is born. When a heart is stirred by a need, that is the moment when God imparts a vision to meet the need.

5. Seek a divine diagnosis: what is the ISSUE TO BE RESOLVED?

The harvest is plentiful but the workers are few (9:37).

Jesus saw the need: the people needed physical, emotional and spiritual healing. And then He identified the problem: there were not enough people to bring them the message of hope and healing. Jesus had been doing the work of healing by Himself up until this point. But there were more people with needs than He was able to touch. His diagnosis: big harvest, few workers.

6. PRAY to determine what action could meet that need.

Ask the Lord of the harvest, therefore, to send out workers into harvest field (9:38).

So what did Jesus determine would meet the need? More workers! And that's what He prayed for. Notice that He didn't pray for bigger buildings or more money. The one action He prayed for was that God would send out more workers.

7. Choose a team and EMPOWER them for partnership.

He called His twelve disciples to Him and gave them authority (10:1).

Without a vision, the people perish. However, there is another truth we must grasp. Without people, a vision perishes. Jesus was not able to care for the needs of the people on His own. That was the problem. He needed more workers to join Him, to help Him fulfill His vision. So He formed a team and empowered them to help Him.

8. TAKE IMMEDIATE ACTION toward the fulfillment of the vision.

These twelve Jesus sent out (10:5).

Jesus doesn't hesitate a bit. He chooses a team and immediately sends them out with instructions on how to carry out His work. He imparts the vision and equips them with the tools to fulfill it. They become the answer to His prayer request for more workers.

What Voice Inspires Your Vision?

As you think about the vision you might pursue, remember that God uses a variety of "voices" to communicate with us. Consider how He has motivated you in the past. What methods has He used?

1. **The Inner Voice:** Does your vision come from life goals, mission statements, or your personal desires? You won't accomplish something you don't believe in.

2. **The Angry Voice:** Does your vision come from dislike of a certain injustice or problem? Do you complain about the darkness or light a match?

3. **The Successful Voice:** Do you find your vision in people who have already gone through the same situation? Find someone who can be a mentor figure in your life.

4. **The Higher Voice:** A truly valuable vision is given from God. Look from the past to guide your present and future. Are you a big-picture person, or do you live life looking through a keyhole?

Contagious Leadership Workbook

Tools to Cast Your Vision . . .

Once you've captured the vision, you must find ways to communicate it to your people. More than fifty years ago, Winston Churchill was a master at communicating vision to the British people during World War II. As Prime Minister, he developed a pattern that he used each time he communicated vision to his people. Here are the five tools he utilized:

TOOL ONE: **Strong Beginning**
(Capture their attention)

TOOL TWO: **One Theme**
(Stay focused)

TOOL THREE: **Simple Language**
(Easy to understand)

TOOL FOUR: **Word Pictures**
(Stories and illustrations)

TOOL FIVE: **Emotional Ending**
(A compelling conclusion)

Conclusion: How We Must Handle Vision

1. See it CLEARLY.

2. Show it CREATIVELY.

3. Say it CONSTANTLY.

ACTION PLAN

ASSESSMENT: What has been your most difficult step as you've attempted to implement vision?

_____

_____

_____

_____

_____

APPLICATION: How can you communicate your vision more effectively and biblically? What are some ways that you can create an environment where you can effectively capture and implement a God-given vision?

_____

_____

_____

_____

_____

Priorities and Decision Making

Lesson 4
Making the Most of Your Time

BIBLICAL BASIS

You blind guides! You strain out a gnat but swallow a camel. (Matt. 23:24 NIV)

Mistaken priorities lie at the heart of ineffective leadership. In Matthew 23:24 Jesus scolded the Pharisees for confusing what was and wasn't important. Their priorities were enforcing laws and rules. Christ's priorities were the spiritual needs of others. Great leaders know the hearts of their people, and they act with the end in mind.

As spiritual leaders we know that Jesus died for us and that our ultimate mission is the Great Commission. We also know that the Bible rarely gives us step-by-step instructions for a given task. Consequently, we must ask God for wisdom, keep the big picture in mind, lead from God's priorities, and make the most of our time since the days are evil (Eph. 5:15–16).

Biblical Answers on Priorities . . .

EXAMINE THE WORD

What Was Jesus's Priority? — Mark 1:35–38 NIV

Very early in the morning, while it was still dark, Jesus got up, left the house and went off to a solitary place, where he prayed. Simon and his companions went to look for him, and when they found him they exclaimed: "Everyone is looking for You!" Jesus

53

replied, "Let us go somewhere else — to the nearby villages — so I can preach there also. That is why I have come."

What Is the Christian's Priority? — Luke 10:38–42 NIV

As Jesus and his disciples were on their way, he came to a village where a woman named Martha opened her home to him. She had a sister called Mary, who sat at the Lord's feet listening to what he said. But Martha was distracted by all the preparations that had to be made. She came to him and asked, "Lord, don't You care that my sister has left me to do the work by myself? Tell her to help me!"

"Martha, Martha," the Lord answered, "you are worried and upset about many things, but only one thing is needed. Mary has chosen what is better, and it will not be taken away from her."

What Is the Priority of Church Leaders? — Acts 6:2–4 NIV

So the Twelve gathered all the disciples together and said, "It would not be right for us to neglect the ministry of the word of God in order to wait on tables. Brothers, choose seven men from among you who are known to be full of the Spirit and wisdom. We will turn this responsibility over to them and will give our attention to prayer and the ministry of the word."

What about Distractions and Hindrances? — Hebrews 12:1 NIV

Let us throw off everything that hinders and the sin that so easily entangles, and let us run with perseverance the race marked out for us. Let us fix our eyes on Jesus . . .

**How Does Our Purpose Help Us with Our Priorities? —
1 Corinthians 9:24–27 NIV**

*Do you not know that in a race all the runners run, but only
one gets the prize? Run in such a way as to get the prize.
Everyone who competes in the games goes into strict training.
They do it to get a crown that will not last; but we do it to get
æa crown that will last forever. Therefore I do not run like a
man running aimlessly; I do not fight like a man beating the air.
No, I beat my body and make it my slave so that after I have
preached to others, I myself will not be disqualified for the prize.*

The 80/20 Principle

The 80/20 Principle teaches us that
if we focus our attention on our most
important activities, we gain the
highest return on our effort. In fact,
if we tend to the top 20 percent of
our most important priorities, we will
accomplish 80 percent of the results
we desire. The principle can be
applied to your everyday life to enable
you to lead more effectively.

Priorities   Results

**TRUTH
IN A
PICTURE**

Take a look at this diagram
on the right. The column on the
left represents your "to do" list.
Accomplishing your first two
priorities will give you 80 percent
of your desired results. This occurs
because you have made the list in the
order of priority. Many of the lower ones are much less fruitful
for the kingdom. They're not priorities you should focus on.

If you embrace the wrong priorities, this principle will work against you — focusing on the bottom 80 percent of your priorities will gain you 20 percent of the results and fruit you desire.

Teach us to number our days aright, that we may gain a heart of wisdom. (Ps. 90:12 NIV)

Examples of the 80/20 Principle

- **Time:** 20 percent of our time produces 80 percent of the results.

- **Counseling:** 20 percent of our clients take up 80 percent of our time.

- **Work:** 20 percent of our effort gives us 80 percent of our satisfaction.

- **Ministries:** 20 percent of all ministries provide 80 percent of all fruit.

- **Leadership:** 20 percent of all people make 80 percent of all decisions.

- **Workers:** 20 percent of all members do 80 percent of the ministry.

- **Mentoring:** 20 percent of the influencers are where you should invest 80 percent your time.

Lessons Learned from the 80/20 Principle

KEY
POINTS

1. **ACTIVITY does not equal accomplishment**: Your goal should not be simply to stay busy. Look for the wisest people and places to invest your time.

2. **Work SMARTER, not HARDER:** Working smarter means working on what you can do, and delegating things others can do. What good is it to work extremely hard when it accomplishes little?

3. **ORGANIZE or agonize:** If you can learn to organize, then you can become more efficient in getting things done. This in turn will save you a lot of time and frustration.

4. **EVALUATE or stagnate:** Determining where you stand in relation to your goal is very important. To move to the next level of leadership, you must evaluate your current situation.

5. **SCHEDULE your priorities:** Control your day or your day will control you! Don't fill your day filling the requests of others. The issue is not prioritizing your schedule, but scheduling your priorities.

6. **REACTING is not leading:** When you lose control you are no longer acting as a leader, but instead reacting to the urgent. If you forget the ultimate, you will become a slave to the immediate.

7. **Say NO to little things:** Leaders must say no to the little things so they can say yes to the big things. If someone else can do it, delegate it!

How To Say No Gracefully . . .

When we know who we are, what our gifts are, and what our calling is, it's much easier to determine the yes's and no's of life. When a task would not further your goal, you need to just say no. The way you say no is just as important as deciding to say it.

1. **Say no to the IDEA — not to the person.**

   Make sure people understand that you are not rejecting them. You're simply saying no to what they want you to do. Give their ideas affirmation, but explain that they don't fit in with the goals that you need to accomplish.

2. **Respond in terms of the BEST INTEREST of the person asking.**

   Make sure people know that you're not just choosing the easy response, but that you want to genuinely help them. Communicate that your time constraints would actually prevent you from doing the kind of work they deserve.

3. **Defer CREATIVELY. Come up with an alternative.**

   Think of a way that helps them complete their task. Give them confidence that they can do it, or maybe help them find someone who will. This will aid them in solving their problem.

On Making the Most of Your Time . . .

PLAN YOUR IMPACT

1. **Make TO DO lists:** Write out what you want to accomplish.

2. **Set your PRIORITIES:** Put the most important items at the top of the list.

3. **Avoid PERFECTIONISM:** Do things with excellence, but perfectionism may be an extreme that you need to avoid if it takes too much time.

4. **QUESTION everything:** Don't allow habits or emotion to keep you from eliminating items from your calendar and "to do" lists. If it doesn't work, get rid of it.

5. **Welcome TENSION:** Don't let stress paralyze you. Let it move you to your goal. Many times tension can help improve your focus and enable you to do the job more effectively.

6. **Avoid CLUTTER:** Clutter will get in the way of what you are doing. By putting everything in its proper place, you won't waste time searching for things.

7. **Avoid PROCRASTINATION:** Priorities come first. Easy things and fun things come afterwards.

8. **Control INTERRUPTIONS and DISTRACTIONS:** Minimize the amount of time that people take away from your main objective.

9. **Staff your WEAKNESSES:** Know your strengths, as a leader, and employ staff members or volunteers who are gifted in the areas of your weaknesses. This is the beauty of the body of Christ.

10. **Use a CALENDAR:** Organizing your days will help save time and prioritize tasks.

CHECK YOUR HEART

Self Evaluation: Three Wise Questions . . .

REQUIREMENT: **What is REQUIRED of me?**

When you feel overwhelmed by obligations, stop and sort out your "must do's" from your "choose to do's." Our obligations in life are the biggest priorities we have, but more often than not, you will find that you really do not *have* to do many things; you *choose* to do them. Simply ask: What must I do? What is truly required of me?

_____

_____

_____

RESULTS: **What gives the greatest RETURN?**

When sorting out priorities, ask the question: What gives me the greatest results? You should spend most of your time working in the area of your greatest strength. A wise person wastes no energy on pursuits for which he or she is not fitted. Find your gift and capitalize your time using it. What activities achieve the most results when you do them?

_____

_____

_____

REWARD: **What gives me the greatest REWARD?**

Finally, as you sort through personal priorities, look for the element of personal fulfillment. God provides deep satisfaction when you do what He has gifted and called you to do. Nothing is easier than neglecting the things you don't want to do. As you draw closer to your God-given mission, you will experience deeper fulfillment. Where do you find your greatest rewards?

Write Down Your Top 20 Percent

Think back to the 80/20 Principle. Remember: Activity does not equal accomplishment. Answer the following questions based on your own leadership strengths and priorities:

Who are the top 20 percent of influential people into whom you should pour your life?

Contagious Leadership Workbook

What activities result in the greatest amount of fruit for you as a leader?

_____

_____

_____

Which of your leadership roles produces the deepest amount of personal fulfillment?

_____

_____

_____

Who are the potential leaders around you whom you can equip for ministry or leadership?

_____

_____

_____

What are other priorities you should pursue as you endeavor to lead people?

_____

_____

_____

Cultivating People Skills in Your Leadership

Lesson 5

The Vital Role of Relationships in Leadership

For I have given you an example, that you should do as I have done to you. (John 13:15 NKJV)

Clearly, no one exemplified people skills better than Jesus, Himself. Everywhere He went people followed Him. Why? Because it was obvious that people were His passion. He met their needs wherever He encountered them. Jesus touched people physically, spiritually, and emotionally.

The basis of leadership is passion for people. An old proverb states, "He who thinks he leads, but has no followers, is only taking a walk." If you can't relate with people, they won't follow you. Relationships will make or break a leader over time. Effective leaders don't focus on themselves and their own success; they are others-minded. To them, success means developing people.

Four Truths about Leadership and People

1. People are a church's most appreciable ASSET.

2. A leader's most important asset is PEOPLE SKILLS.

3. A good leader can lead various groups because leadership is about PEOPLE.

65

Contagious Leadership Workbook

4. You can have people skills and not be a good LEADER, but you cannot be a good leader without people skills.

LUKE 10:30–37

Jesus told this story in response to a man who asked, "Who is my neighbor?" He spoke of a man who was robbed and beaten alongside a road and left for dead. Soon, a couple of religious leaders walked by but never stopped. It is likely they were on their way to some religious activity. Then, a Samaritan came by and helped the man, caring for him until he was well again. Jesus then asked: Who was the neighbor in this story? He taught that relationships and ministry are not confined to your immediate circle of friends (Luke 10:36–37). He taught that relationships are more important than many spiritual activities we practice (Matt. 5:23–24). He also taught the truth below.

The Way You See Yourself Is the Way You Serve Your People

The story of the "Good Samaritan" illustrates how we treat others based upon how we see ourselves. Notice the different ways the victimized man was treated in this story . . .

1. **The Robbers**

   They used people.

   They manipulated others.

   They saw the man as a VICTIM TO EXPLOIT.

2. **The Priests:**

   They were law keepers.

   They were pure.

   They saw the man as a PROBLEM TO AVOID.

66

3. **The Samaritan:**

> He was despised.
>
> He knew how it felt to be ignored.
>
> He saw the man as a PERSON TO BE LOVED.

As a leader, you will be tempted to do all three of these in your ministry — exploit, avoid, and love — people. The goal is to look past their faults and see their needs.

Leadership Is Relationships

Years ago, several Christian leaders met together in a summit. Their goal was to summarize the Christian faith into a single sentence. They actually took the goal a step further. They summarized Christianity into a single word. The one word they chose . . .

Christianity is *Relationships*

What separates us from all other religions in the world is the centrality of relationships. Our faith is built around relationships, not creeds or disciplines. Consider this: When Jesus was asked about the greatest commandment, He said we're to "love the Lord with all of our heart, mind, soul, and strength" (a vertical relationship) and "to love our neighbor as ourselves" (a horizontal relationship). Jesus did not say: By this will all men know that you are my disciples — that you have memorized fifty verses of Scripture. Instead, He said that the way the world would know we are His disciples is how we handle our relationships. How well do we love people?

CHECK YOUR HEART

Question: Think of the people in your life who are the most difficult to love. Why are they difficult to love? How do you view them?

_____

_____

_____

Question: How can you begin to see people the way the Samaritan saw the man?

_____

_____

_____

People don't care how much you know,
until they know how much you care.
—Dr. John C. Maxwell

A Definition for Spiritual Leadership:

ONE WHO ASSUMES RESPONSIBILITY FOR THE HEALTH AND DEVELOPMENT OF HIS RELATIONSHIPS

Four Word Pictures

1. **The analogy of the HOST:** Good hosts take initiative and make others feel comfortable.

   As a leader, you must "host" the relationships and conversations of your life. Leaders are not guests in relationships. Knowing what a good host does in his home, we ought to practice the same principles with people everywhere.
      Many leaders make the mistake of separating leadership from relationships. This happens when a person steps into a position of leadership and assumes that everyone will follow them because of their position.

2. **The analogy of the DOCTOR:** Good doctors ask questions. They probe until they see the need.

   As you attempt to discern people's needs, ask questions until you discern their condition. Only then do you try to address their needs. Don't give a prescription before a diagnosis.

3. **The analogy of the COUNSELOR:** Good counselors are active listeners and interpret what they hear.

   As a leader with solid people skills, you must become an active listener. You should non-verbally communicate that you understand the person to whom you are listening and identify with him/her. We earn our right to speak by listening.

4. **The analogy of the TOUR GUIDE:** Guides don't merely fellowship with others; they get them to the destination.

   A leader's people skills must result in his ability to take people to a destination. Our purpose is not to be liked by

Contagious Leadership Workbook

people, but to take them on a journey and to reach a goal they might not have reached alone.

A leader should take the appropriate role according to the needs the person they are leading. Our job is to "connect" with people, so that we can take them on the journey.

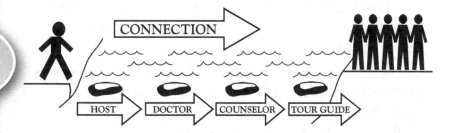

What Every Leader Should Know about People . . .

1. **People are INSECURE. Give them confidence.**

   Key Principle: Hurting people hurt people. Secure people offer security to people.

   a. Most people are insecure in some area of their life.

   b. Most insecure people are looking for security.

   c. A secure environment is provided only by secure and confident people.

   Let us encourage one another. (Heb. 10:25 NIV)

2. **People like to feel SPECIAL. Honor them.**

   Key Principle: To deal with yourself, use your head. To deal with others, use your heart.

When You Affirm and Honor Someone with Your Words . . .

a. **Make them *sincere.*** Be genuine about what you say.

b. **Make them *specific*.** Be pointed and specific about what you say.

c. **Make them *public*.** Share the honoring word in front of others.

d. **Make them *personal*.** Get beyond general gratitude; speak personally to the individual.

Be kindly affectionate to one another with brotherly love, in honor giving preference to one another. (Rom. 12:10 NKJV)

3. **People look for a better TOMORROW. Give them hope.**

   Key Principle: The key to today is a belief in tomorrow.

   Everyone lives for something better to come. Where there is no hope in the future, there is no power in the present. Years ago a study was done to see what effective pastors had in common. They had one common characteristic: Each of them said that their main goal every Sunday was to offer hope to their people.

   Yet I still dare to hope when I remember this: The unfailing love of the LORD never ends! . . . Great is his faithfulness; his mercies begin afresh each day. (Lam. 3:21–23 NLT)

4. **People need to be UNDERSTOOD. Listen to them.**

   Key Principle: To connect with others, understand the "keys" to their heart.

   Knowing the key to people's hearts:

   a. What do they *talk* about?

   b. What do they *cry* about?

71

Contagious Leadership Workbook

   c. What do they *dream* about?

   d. What do they *laugh* about?

   e. What do they *plan* about?

Rejoice with those who rejoice, and weep with those who weep. (Rom. 12:15 NKJV)

5. **People lack DIRECTION. Navigate for them.**

  Key Principle: Most people can steer the ship; a leader helps chart the course.

   a. Leaders must *know* the way.

   b. Leaders must *go* the way.

   c. Leaders must *show* the way.

The elders who are among you I exhort, I who am a fellow elder and a witness of the sufferings of Christ, and also a partaker of the glory that will be revealed: Shepherd the flock of God which is among you, serving as overseers, not by compulsion but willingly, not for dishonest gain but eagerly . . . (1 Pet. 5:1–2 NKJV)

6. **People are NEEDY. Speak to their needs first.**

  Key Principle: People must be ministered to before they can minister.

Most people think . . .	*Leaders must . . .*
Their situation is unique.	Put their people first.
Their problems are the biggest.	Know their people's needs.
Their faults should be overlooked.	See the total picture.
Their time is most precious.	Love people to help them grow.

Let each of you look out not only for his own interests, but also for the interests of others. (Phil. 2:4 NKJV)

7. **People get EMOTIONALLY LOW. Encourage them.**

   Key Principle: What gets rewarded, gets done.

   An Experiment . . .

   Years ago, an experiment was conducted to measure people's capacity to endure pain. How long could a bare-footed person stand in a bucket of ice water? It was discovered that when there was someone else present offering encouragement and support, the person standing in the ice water could tolerate the pain twice as long as when there was no one present.

   . . . put on tender mercies, kindness, humility, meekness, longsuffering; bearing with one another. (Col. 3:12b–13a NKJV)

8. **People want to SUCCEED. Help them win.**

Key Principle: Reach out and help others achieve their goals. Victory has a thousand fathers, defeat is an orphan.

Question: What do these words have in common?

High morale	Enthusiasm	Momentum
Optimism	Energy	Excitement

Answer: Victory. Everyone wants to be on a team that experiences victories and reaches the goal they are pursuing. Leaders provide this for others.

Two are better than one, Because they have a good reward for their labor. For if they fall, one will lift up his companion. (Eccles. 4: 9–10a NKJV)

9. **People desire RELATIONSHIPS. Provide community.**

Key Principle: Practice the 101 Percent Principle with people: Find the 1 percent you have in common with someone, and give it 100 percent of your attention.

God's Word is all about community — from the Garden of Eden in the beginning, to the city of God in the end. We were never intended to take the Christian journey alone. The New Testament teaches us "we are members of one another." The word "saint" (in the singular form) does not appear once, in the New Testament. The word "saints" (in the plural form) appears many times.

And if one member suffers, all the members suffer with it; or if one member is honored, all the members rejoice with it. (1 Cor. 12:26 NKJV)

10. **People seek MODELS to follow. Be an example.**

Key Principle: People do what people see.

A Life Example: The early followers of St. Francis of Assisi wanted to know what to do when they went out into the streets to minister. "Preach the gospel at all times," St. Francis advised. "If necessary, use words."

And you should follow my example, just as I follow Christ. (1 Cor. 11:1 NLT)

ASSESSMENT: What do you struggle with most in relationships? Now, list some people whom you believe God is challenging you to host and lead more effectively.

ACTION PLAN

APPLICATION: How can you begin to overcome these struggles, and connect with these people?

Strategic Planning

Lesson 6

Failing to Plan Is a Plan to Fail

Give me wisdom and knowledge, that I may
lead this people, for who is able to govern
this great people of yours?
(2 Chron. 1:10 NIV)

The key to great planning is *focus*. Solomon did not ask for great riches or fame for himself, but rather he asked for wisdom so that he could lead God's people. Solomon demonstrates a key aspect of leadership — knowing where you want to go before asking others to follow you. Once your personal and organizational mission is defined, the methods become easier to clarify as well. All great human endeavors have included a God factor and a leadership factor. God has given us a mission that requires planning on our part as leaders.

Accomplishing the Mission

Do I have complete knowledge of my mission?	Yes	Maybe	No
Do I have complete knowledge of my capabilities?	Yes	Maybe	No
Do I have complete knowledge of my team's capabilities?	Yes	Maybe	No

77

Do I receive constant feedback and open communications?	Yes	Maybe	No

Do I use this information to adapt and change when necessary?	Yes	Maybe	No

Question: What is my mission?

_____

_____

_____

Question: What has hindered me from accomplishing this mission?

_____

_____

_____

Biblical Examples of Planning

God Did It . . .

EXAMINE THE WORD

Have you not heard? Long ago I did it, from ancient times I planned it. Now I have brought it to pass . . . . (Isa. 37:26 NASB)

Noah Did It . . .

Noah received explicit instructions from God to build the ark. God gave detailed measurements to Noah, and Noah was faithful to carry out the long-range plan. He finished construction of the ark, exactly as God told him — in 120 years. The ark was built so well that it withstood forty days of torrential rain, and then it floated a solid year as the floods subsided. (Gen. 7–9)

Nehemiah Did It . . .

The long-range plan of Nehemiah was to see the wall of Jerusalem rebuilt. He visualized the completion of the wall and then began plans for its construction. The work was completed in fifty-two days because each family was assigned a certain portion of the wall to build. He planned and organized the project with excellence. (Neh. 1–5)

David Did It . . .

The long-range plan of David was to build a temple (2 Sam. 7). God did not allow David to build it because of his associations with wars (1 Kings 5:2–3). However, when Solomon was chosen to succeed him, David handed Solomon the completed plan for the temple and a list of materials on hand. After seven years of construction, the temple was completed, and the long-range plan of David was fulfilled.

Jesus Told Parables about It . . .

We often fail to notice that Jesus frequently spoke about the necessity of planning and strategy. In many of His parables, He explained how foolish it is to neglect planning:

- **The Wise and Foolish Builder:** Matthew 7:24–27

- **The Builder Counting the Cost:** Luke 14:28–30

- **The King Planning for Battle:** Luke 14:31–32

- **The Unjust Steward:** Luke 16:1–8

TRUTH IN A PICTURE

The Changing Future

The Growth Curve . . .

Charles Handy writes that most organizational growth occurs as the diagram illustrates to the right. Growth comes quickly (point A) but eventually peaks, and then decline sets in (point B). A leader must understand this, and make changes before the decline sets in. This means that a leader must begin change at point A.

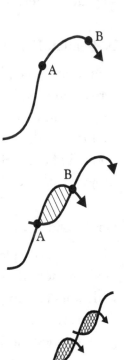

Anticipating Change and the Period of Chaos . . .

When change is initiated at point A, the followers will misunderstand what the leader is doing. When the change is made they often feel upset, resentful and in a state of flux. This is the "period of chaos" (the shaded area).

Thriving on Chaos . . .

Because of the rapid change of pace in an organization, the leader must constantly be evaluating, planning and making healthy changes. This means followers may feel unsettled like they're in a constant state of chaos. Great leaders and organizations must learn to thrive on this.

Application . . .

Leaders must prepare their followers for the period of chaos early in the long-term planning process. Followers must be continually informed of what is going on *in advance* of the implementation of any plans. Gain the trust of followers by including them in the plans, giving them ownership of their part, and encouraging them through periods of chaos.

Steps to Effective Strategic Planning

1. **Plan to PLAN.**

   A frequent mistake churches make is failing to follow this step. A certain amount of time and energy must be allotted in the weekly agenda for the planning process. Everyone agrees that strategic planning is important, but we often feel we're wasting time when we take long hours to do it. The opposite is usually true. Look at the diagram below. When very little planning happens it takes more time for execution due to changes and unexpected events. When a good deal of time is spent planning, we may feel unproductive, but in the long run we will actually save time on the overall task. The graph below is not a scientific formula, but rather a picture of what can happen when we spend time planning our actions.

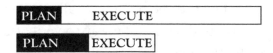

2. **Determine your PRIMARY PURPOSE.**

   This involves big-picture perspective. Before you can decide on daily agendas, you must determine what goal you want to reach. Strategic planning (long-term) and operational planning (short-term) both flow out of the answers to these questions:

Why do we exist?

_____

_____

_____

_____

What are we trying to accomplish?

_____

_____

_____

_____

3. **ASSESS the situation.**

   A plan for the future based on an unrealistic view of the present will lead to disaster. One way to verify that we are seeing the situation clearly is to look at it from different angles. Take our eyes for example. Two eyes give depth perception because each eye sees the picture from a different angle. In the same way we can have a clearer idea of our present situation when we look at it from more than one angle. Listed below are four angles to consider when assessing your situation.

– *Angles of Assessment* –

a. INSIDE the Organization

What are you doing from the perspective of those with whom you work?

b. OUTSIDE the Organization

What are you doing from the perspective of someone who does not know your strategy?

c. CURRENT Point of View

What does your situation look like from where you are now?

d. FUTURE Point of View

How does your situation look months or years from now? What *trends* are developing?

4. **PRIORITIZE the needs.**

List team goals in the order of importance and priority. Results are left to chance when needs are not prioritized. More often than not, the easy things will get done, but the important things will not. We tend to do the urgent things but not the important ones. When the ultimate mission is neglected, we become a slave to the immediate.

5. **Ask the right QUESTIONS.**

- **Target:** Whom are we trying to serve and what needs are we meeting?

- **Leadership:** Do we have the right people at the top to accomplish our goals?

- **Counsel:** Whose advice do we need in order to succeed?

- **Direction:** Exactly what are we going to do short-range, mid-range, and long-range?

83

- **Organization:** Who's responsible for what? Who will supervise whom?

- **Funding:** What are our expected expenses and income?

- **Reporting:** Are we on target with our progress?

- **Communication:** How can we effectively make known what we're doing?

- **Evaluating:** Are we seeking the quality we expect or demand from ourselves?

- **Refining:** How can we keep improving in the critical aspects of this ministry?

6. **Set specific GOALS.**

Written

Write out on paper what you want to accomplish. It will serve as a daily reminder of what should be completed next.

Specific

A general plan may be easy to formulate, but objectives are easier to define when the goal is specific.

Realistic

Set goals you can reach. Though it may be exhilarating at first when you set lofty goals, we need to remember that a goal is only worthwhile if it is completed.

Measurable

A measurable goal is important because it allows you to evaluate how well you are doing.

Personal

Personal goals inspire and motivate you. They need to connect at the heart level and move you to act.

Convictional

You must be convinced of the worthiness of your goals. Only then will you invest in them.

7. **COMMUNICATE and clarify.**

Communication is sharing a vision of the objective that is to be accomplished. Clarification is showing the steps that need to be followed. This does not mean specifically telling someone what to do. Instead, it means giving him or her guidelines for completing the goal. Every planning meeting should include the items below.

a. Written conclusion

b. Project list

c. Time-line

d. Resource list

e. Next steps (action items)

f. Responsibility (project leaders)

8. **Identify possible OBSTACLES.**

The next step is identifying possible challenges. Think of obstacles that might occur so you can develop ways to overcome them. Imagine a "worst case scenario" and how you would respond. With planning and forethought, you can avoid many of the obstacles that would normally take up your time. When you take the time to plan, it will take less time to execute.

a. **The Mental Walk Through:** Mentally walk through the entire goal or event you are planning and note anything you might have forgotten.

b. **The Next Steps:** Determine the immediate action you must take to accomplish your goal. This is the most important result of any meeting.

9. **Have an OPEN SYSTEM of planning.**

Leaders must have an open-system approach to planning that is aware of external influences. The decision making and planning can adapt to these realities. A closed system attempts to exist with no regard to these outside factors.

10. **MANAGE and DIRECT your resources.**

Other than people, your most valuable assets are time (schedule) and money (budget). Invest in both wisely and specifically.

Schedule
Put your items on a schedule that is responsible yet productive. Without a schedule, you can't keep on track.

Budget
Determine the cost of the project and at what point costs will be incurred. Attempt to remove any surprises you possibly can!

11. **MONITOR and CORRECT.**

A river constantly changes and is never the same as it was before. Organizations are the same way. Regardless of how conscientiously plans are made, there is a constant need for monitoring and correction if the final destination is to be reached. Always have a plan, but have the understanding that the minute you stop adjusting and making changes your course will be altered and you will get off track.

12. **STUDY the results.**

"Keeping score" is the only way to know if you're winning or losing. Develop vehicles to keep score. If you're making a change, you ought to do it based on current information.

ACTION PLAN

ASSESSMENT: What ministry idea is foremost in your priorities right now?

_____

_____

_____

_____

_____

ACTION: Use the space below to begin the planning process for this project.

_____

_____

_____

_____

_____

_____

The Leadership Test

Lesson 7

Life's Tests Reveal a Leader's Potential and Maturity

BIBLICAL BASIS

Examine me, O LORD, and try me;
Test my mind and my heart. (Ps. 26:2 NASB)

Nearly every moment of life is a test. However, there are "seasons of testing" that can be identified, understood, and passed if we are alert. Leaders experience greater scrutiny, testing, and judgment than followers do, according to James 3:1.

Think about it. Tests are common to all of us. Tests are given consistently in schools. Many products and appliances are tested before they are sold. Nearly every part of a new car is taken through intensive tests for safety and performance. When God tests leaders, He takes them through a crucial screening which reveals what they are made of. Passing the test is the pathway to progress and promotion.

A Definition of Testing

AN OPPORTUNITY WHICH CHALLENGES LEADERS TO DEMONSTRATE THEIR POTENTIAL AND MATURITY

Contagious Leadership Workbook

Tests Reveal Three Truths

1. **INWARD POVERTY:** The test reveals you have responded poorly at an increasing rate and you have failed to act obediently.

2. **INWARD PLATEAU:** The test reveals you have not matured, but have become stagnant in your growth.

3. **INWARD PROGRESS:** The test reveals you have grown and have responded better than ever.

Question: Think of a test you have experienced recently. How did you respond?

_____

_____

_____

Question: What have your recent tests revealed: poverty, plateau, or progress?

_____

_____

_____

Genesis 22:1–2, 9–13

In this passage, Abraham is ushered into a "test of faith" to reveal the content of his heart. It is clear from the passage, as well as from commentary in the New Testament book of Hebrews, that God did not intend to have Isaac executed.

It was merely a test for his father, a test that he passed successfully, proving he had settled the issues of obedience and Lordship.

David, one of Israel's greatest leaders, welcomed these tests in his leadership. Listen to his insight and note how aware he was of the need for testing:

Psalm 7:9 NKJV

... For the righteous God tests the hearts and minds.

Psalm 17:3 NIV

Though you probe my heart and examine me at night, though you test me, you will find nothing; I have resolved that my mouth will not sin.

Psalm 26:2 NKJV

Examine me, O Lord, and prove me; try my mind and my heart.

Psalm 139:23–24 NASB

Search me, O God, and know my heart; try me and know my anxious thoughts; and see if there be any hurtful way in me, and lead me in the everlasting way.

Clearly, tests are our friends. Leaders should welcome them. They tell us the truth when other friends cannot or will not be so blunt. The apostle Paul closes his final letter to the Corinthians with some sobering words:

Test yourselves to see if you are in the faith; examine yourselves! (2 Cor. 13:5a NASB)

Observe the positive result of tests from the book of James:

Contagious Leadership Workbook

Consider it pure joy, my brothers, whenever you face trials of many kinds, because you know that the testing of your faith develops perseverance. Perseverance must finish its work so that you may be mature and complete, not lacking anything. (James 1:2–4 NIV)

The Truth about Testing

1. WE ALL EXPERIENCE TESTS AT EACH STAGE OF OUR GROWTH.

2. OUR GOAL SHOULD BE TO PASS EVERY TEST.

3. TESTING ALWAYS PRECEDES PROMOTION.

4. SELF-PROMOTION AND HUMAN PROMOTION CAN'T REPLACE DIVINE PROMOTION.

5. JUST AS A PRODUCT IS NEVER USED UNTIL IT'S TESTED — SO IT IS WITH US.

TRUTH IN A PICTURE

PROMOTION: Growth Becomes Visible

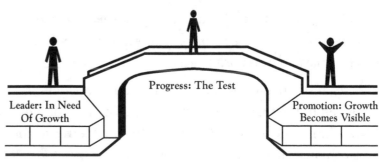

Progress: The Test

Leader: In Need Of Growth

Promotion: Growth Becomes Visible

Ten Tests That Prove Leadership Potential and Maturity

1. **TEST OF SMALL THINGS:** This test comes to prove our faithfulness and potential for greater opportunities.

   … making the most of every opportunity, because the days are evil. (Eph. 5:16 NIV)

   He who is faithful in a very little thing is faithful also in much; and he who is unrighteous in a very little thing is unrighteous also in much. (Luke 16:10 NASB)

2. **MOTIVATION TEST:** This test comes to the one who is doing right, to examine *why* they are doing it.

   Then Satan answered the LORD, "Does Job fear God for nothing? Have You not made a hedge about him and his house and all that he has, on every side? You have blessed the work of his hands, and his possessions have increased in the land. But put forth Your hand now and touch all that he has; he will surely curse You to Your face." (Job 1:9–11 NASB)

3. **STEWARDSHIP TEST:** This test proves how strategically and generously we handle the resources we presently control.

   And then He told them this parable: "The ground of a certain rich man produced a good crop. He thought to himself, 'What shall I do? I have no place to store my crops.' Then he said, 'This is what I'll do. I will tear down my barns and build bigger ones, and there I will store all my grain and my goods. And I'll say to myself, "You have plenty of good things laid up for many years. Take life easy; eat, drink and be merry."' But God said to him: 'You fool! This very night your life will be demanded from you; Then who will get what you have prepared for

*yourself?' This is how it will be with anyone who stores
up things for himself but is not rich toward God."*
(Luke 12:16–21 NIV)

*His master said to him, "Well done, good and faithful slave;
you were faithful with a few things, I will put you in charge of
many things . . . "* (Matt. 25:21 NASB)

4. **WILDERNESS TEST:** This test comes when you're
spiritually dry to reveal your potential for change and
growth.

*He led you through the great and terrible wilderness, with
its fiery serpents and scorpions and thirsty ground where
there was no water... In the wilderness, He fed you manna
which your fathers did not know, that He might humble you
and that He might test you, to do good for you, in the end.*
(Deut. 8:15–16 NASB)

5. **CREDIBILITY TEST:** This test displays our ability and
integrity — to see if we compromise under pressure.

*But when Cephas came to Antioch, I opposed him to his face,
because he stood condemned. For prior to the coming of certain
men from James, he used to eat with the Gentiles; but when
they came, he began to withdraw and hold himself aloof, fearing
the party of the circumcision. The rest of the Jews joined him in
hypocrisy, with the result that even Barnabas was carried away
by their hypocrisy.* (Gal. 2:11–13 NASB)

*But the LORD said to Samuel, "Do not look at his appearance
or at the height of his stature, because I have rejected him;
for God sees not as a man sees, for man looks at the outward
appearance, but the LORD looks at the heart."* (1 Sam. 16:7
NASB)

6. **AUTHORITY TEST**: This test comes to expose your attitude and willing submission toward God-given authority.

Then Saul took three thousand chosen men from all Israel, and went to seek David and his men in front of the Rocks of the Wild Goats . . . The men of David said to him, "Behold, this is the day the Lord said to you, 'Behold; I am about to give your enemy into your hand'" . . . So he said to his men, "Far be it from me because of the LORD *that I should do this thing to my lord, the* LORD's *anointed, to stretch out my hand against him, since he is the* LORD's *anointed." David persuaded his men . . . and did not allow them to rise up against Saul.* (1 Sam. 24:2,4,6–7 NASB)

7. **FORGIVENESS TEST**: This test comes to show you're not easily offended and are ready to forgive others.

Pursue peace with all men . . . see to it that no one comes short of the grace of God; that no root of bitterness springing up causes trouble, and by it many be defiled . . . (Heb. 12:14–15 NASB)

Whenever you stand praying, forgive, if you have anything against anyone, so that your Father who is in heaven will also forgive you your transgressions. But if you do not forgive, neither will your Father who is in heaven forgive your transgressions. (Mark 11:25–26 NASB)

8. **WARFARE TEST**: This test exposes your ability to stand when you're in God's will and experience adversity.

If they face war, they might change their minds and return to Egypt. (Exod. 13:17 NIV)

If you have run with the footmen and they have tired you out, then how can you compete with horses? If you fall down in a land of peace, how will you do in the thicket of the Jordan? (Jer. 12:5 NASB)

9. **TEST OF TIME:** This test reveals the quality of your work, based on both opportunity and longevity.

For if you remain silent at this time, relief and deliverance will arise for the Jews from another place and you and your father's house will perish. And who knows whether you have not attained royalty for such a time as this? (Esther 4:14 NASB)

And let us not lose heart in doing good, for in due time we will reap if we do not grow weary. (Gal. 6:9 NASB)

10. **LORDSHIP TEST:** This test usually occurs in one of your areas of strength. You find it difficult to trust God. It reveals your heart response to whom or what has the final authority in your life.

When He had finished speaking, He said to Simon, "Put out into the deep water and let down your nets for a catch." Simon answered and said, "Master, we worked hard all night and caught nothing, but I will do as You say and let down the nets." When they had done this, they enclosed a great quantity of fish, and their nets began to break; so they signaled to their partners in the other boat for them to come and help them. (Luke 5:4–7 NASB)

ASSESSMENT: Which of the tests have you experienced this year? Have you passed them?

ACTION
PLAN

_____

_____

_____

_____

APPLICATION: Whatever test you are facing now, write down what you can do to exhibit your trust in God and your credibility to lead effectively.

_____

_____

_____

_____

Security or Sabotage

Lesson 8

How Emotional Insecurity Prevents Effective Leadership

If a ruler listens to lies, all his officials become wicked. (Prov. 29:12 NIV)

One of the greatest tragedies of church life surrounds the insecurities of her leaders. Leadership disasters happen every week while pastors pretend the problem instead lies in theology or programs.

The fact of the matter is, the reason for many unresolved problems within a church is the emotional insecurity of the pastor. The symptoms show up in a variety of ways. The leader may fail to confront a situation. He may lack moral backbone. He may get defensive when others disagree with him. He may withdraw from a leadership function which causes others to question his leadership. He may lack the character to stand up when he isn't liked. Because of this insecurity, the leader begins to believe lies about himself or others and begins to sabotage his own leadership.

Spotting Insecurity in Your Behavior

To be honest, personal insecurity is fairly easy to spot in our behavior. We fail to see it merely because we ignore it. We pretend it isn't there by defending ourselves and diverting the focus to something else. The following are biblical case studies, where ordinary people like you and me struggled with common insecurities of some sort. Notice how it showed up in their lives.

1. **COMPARISON:** You begin to compare yourself to others.

   Danger: You ignore the unique role you and others are to play on the team.

   Example: The Vineyard Workers (Matt. 20)

   a. You ignore God's grace to you because you are preoccupied with the status of others.

   b. You grumble and complain about perceived inequities.

   c. You judge others as less worthy of blessing than you.

   When Peter saw him, he asked "Lord, what about him?" Jesus answered: "If I want him to remain alive until I return, what is that to you? You must follow me." (John 21:21–22 NIV)

2. **COMPENSATION:** You feel like a victim and must compensate for your inferiority.

   Danger: You fail to trust God's control by taking matters into your own hands.

   Example: Jacob (Gen. 27, 32)

   a. You scheme about how to get ahead and how to gain recognition.

   b. You fight irrational battles to get what you think you deserve.

   c. You may stoop to dishonesty and deception to get results.

   Do not fret . . . Be not envious . . . Trust in the LORD and do good; Dwell in the land and cultivate faithfulness. Delight yourself in the LORD, and He will give you the desires of your heart. Commit your way to the LORD, trust also in Him, and He will do it. Rest in the LORD . . . Do not fret . . . Cease from anger. (Ps. 37:1–8 NASB)

3. **COMPETITION:** You drift into self-centered patterns, trying to out-perform others.

   Danger: You become obsessed with building your own kingdom, and you will do anything to win.

   Example: The "Older" Prodigal Son (Luke 15)

   a. You tend to keep score on life.

   b. You tend to be critical and judgmental.

   c. You tend to live a self-centered life.

   But each one must examine his own work, and then he will have reason for boasting in regard to himself alone, and not in regard to another. For each one will bear his own load. (Gal. 6:4–5 NASB)

4. **COMPULSION:** You are driven to gain others' approval; you are a people-pleaser.

   Danger: You risk burnout due to impure motives and unrealistic expectations.

   Example: Martha (Luke 10)

   a. You get distracted from "big picture" priorities, consumed by your own performance.

   b. You grow weary because you attempt to do too much — for the wrong reasons.

   c. You tend to be a perfectionist.

By the grace of God I am what I am, and His grace toward me did not prove vain; but I labored even more than all of them, yet not I, but the grace of God with me. (1 Cor. 15:10 NASB)

5. **CONDEMNATION:** You demonstrate a judgmental attitude of yourself or others.

   Danger: You experience a distortion of reality and are tempted to withdraw from responsibility.

   Example: Elijah (I Kings 19)

   a. You have a shortsighted perception of your circumstances.

   b. You complain about unjust circumstances and feel overwhelmed.

   c. You fear your own demise and insignificance.

But to me it is a very small thing that I may be examined by you, or by any human court; in fact, I do not even examine myself. For I am conscious of nothing against myself, yet I am not by this acquitted; but the one who examines me is the Lord. Therefore do not go on passing judgment before the time, but wait until the Lord comes who will both bring to light the things hidden in the darkness and disclose the motives of men's hearts; and then each man's praise will come to him from God. (1 Cor. 4:3–5 NASB)

6. **CONTROL:** In order to validate your own worth, you feel you must take charge.

Danger: You think win/lose, not win/win. Because you are charting your own course, you risk integrity, protect personal "turf," and often slip into the "scarcity paradigm" of thinking that you never have enough.

Example: Sarah (Gen. 16)

a. Your circumstances determine your understanding of God's character.

b. You become self-seeking and manipulative of others.

c. You eventually suffer from the "martyr" syndrome.

"For I know the plans that I have for you," declares the LORD, *"plans for your welfare and not for calamity to give you a future and a hope. Then you will call upon Me and come and pray to Me, and I will listen to you. You will seek Me and find Me when you search for Me with all your heart."* (Jer. 29:11–13 NASB)

The Lies We Believe

It is possible to experience several of these symptoms at the same time. The key is to identify how you cope with your insecurity and to detect what kind of lies you tell yourself about the reality you face.

Consider this: If the truth makes us free (John 8:32), then lies put us in bondage. The level of defeat and bondage you face as a leader may be directly linked to the volume of myths or lies you have embraced about your identity. Our problem is that while we know the truth . . . we believe the lie. Dr. Chris Thurman has written an insightful book entitled, *The Lies We Believe.* He provides a helpful process for us to understand.

CHECK
YOUR
HEART

Stepping Into the Truth

1. DETERMINE the trigger event that fostered the lie/bondage.

Example: Your supervisor failed to affirm the hard work you put in on last week's successful outreach event. You feel resentful and insignificant.

2. DISCOVER the lie you have believed about that situation.

Example: Perhaps you have embraced the lie: "I am only as good as what I do." You have attached your value to your performance and the approval of others.

3. DECIDE what response is truthful, appropriate and realistic.

Example: My personal worth is tied to who I am, not what I do. My supervisor does appreciate me, but he is human like me and likely failed to notice my work due to an oversight. After all, he has been very busy himself.

Tips and Truths

a. We must never put our emotional health in the hands of someone else.

b. The truth is a requirement for spiritual and emotional health.

c. Most of our unhappiness and insecurity is the result of lies we believe.

d. Recognize that you will believe what you want to believe.

e. The truth can be eclipsed by a thrilling lie.

f. Remember that hurting people naturally hurt people; intimidated people intimidate.

Keys to Emotional Security

1. **IDENTITY:** You must tie your self-worth to your identity in Christ, not to people and performance.

2. **BROKENNESS:** You must allow God to break you from self-sufficiency and self-promotion.

3. **PURPOSE:** You must discover and practice your God-given purpose in life, not someone else's.

4. **GIVING AND RECEIVING "THE BLESSING":** You must learn to let others love and bless you, and do the same for them.

What to Do

1. STUDY and MEDITATE on the Scriptures that define your identity in Christ.

2. Check yourself each time you COMPARE yourself to someone. Pause and thank God for the differences.

3. Focus attention on your STRENGTHS for a season. Identify and polish your gifts and skills.

4. Read and listen to MOTIVATIONAL material: books, tapes, magazines, etc.

Contagious Leadership Workbook

5. Identify the two or three most common LIES you believe about yourself. Write down the truth about those areas, then tell yourself the truth.

6. Find someone who is "safe" to be a SUPPORT person. Practice giving and receiving the love, encouragement, and truth you both need.

7. Watch for VULNERABLE situations: criticism, rejection, meeting someone important, a colleague's success, failure, or unfamiliar territory.

8. Remind yourself of the TRUTH: We are to imitate Christ — Who came and emptied Himself in order to serve others, not to be served.

ASSESSMENT: What symptoms of insecurity have you seen in your leadership?

ACTION PLAN

APPLICATION: What keys must you implement to foster emotional security?

_____

_____

_____

_____

_____

Delegating Tasks and Developing People

Lesson 9

Moving from Addition to Multiplication

*Then the twelve summoned the multitude
of the disciples and said, "It is not desirable that
we should leave the word of God and serve tables.
Therefore, brethren, seek out from among you seven
men of good reputation, full of the Holy Spirit and
wisdom, whom we may appoint over this business."*
(Acts 6:2–3 NKJV)

When ministers decide to become leaders, they take an important stand. They make a revolutionary decision in the way they perform their ministry. They no longer evaluate themselves only by what they can do themselves. Their value now depends on what they can get done through others! This is what we call the "Jethro Principle."

The Day Moses Became a Leader

In Exodus 18:17–27 NASB Jethro introduces this principle to Moses.

> *Moses' father-in-law said to him, "The thing that you are doing is not good. You will surely wear out, both yourself and these people who are with you, for the task is too heavy for you; you cannot do it alone."*

BIBLICAL BASIS

Contagious Leadership Workbook

Jethro proceeded to give Moses wise counsel as to how he could delegate his workload and multiply the amount of service being rendered to others. The Scripture says: "So Moses listened to his father-in-law and did all that he said . . ." (Exod. 18:24 NASB)

Many times, it is easy for the leader to feel as if he or she must accomplish everything alone. However, as Jethro points out, that will cause one to wear out quickly. As a result, Moses made changes and began to equip others to share the responsibilities.

Seven Changes Moses Made to Become a Leader (Exod. 18 NASB)

EXAMINE THE WORD

1. He became a man of PRAYER (v. 19).

Now listen to me: I will give you counsel, and God be with you. You be the people's representative before God, and you bring the disputes to God.

2. He committed himself to COMMUNICATION (v. 20).

Then teach them the statutes and the laws, and make known to them the way in which they are to walk and the work they are to do.

3. He laid out the VISION (v. 20).

Then teach them the statutes and the laws, and make known to them the way in which they are to walk and the work they are to do.

4. He developed a PLAN (v. 20).

Then teach them the statutes and the laws, and make known to them the way in which they are to walk and the work they are to do.

5. He SELECTED and trained the leaders (v. 21).

Furthermore, you shall select out of all the people able men who fear God, men of truth, those who hate dishonest gain; and you shall place these over them as leaders of thousands, of hundreds, of fifties and of tens.

6. He released them to SERVE based on their gifts (v. 22).

Let them judge the people at all times . . . every minor dispute they themselves will judge."

7. He only did what THEY could not do (v. 22).

. . . and let it be that every major dispute they will bring to you . . .

In verse 23, we see the results of Moses's change: strength for Moses and peace for the people.

If you do this thing and God so commands you, then you will be able to endure, and all these people also will go to their place in peace.

CHECK YOUR HEART

From Minister to Leader

There is a difference between a minister and a leader. While every leader is also to be a minister, not every minister is a leader. Look at how they differ:

MINISTER	LEADER
1. Serves people.	1. Serves people.
2. Directly meets the needs of people.	2. Empowers others to meet the needs of people.
3. Draws fulfillment from doing the work.	3. Draws fulfillment from equipping others to do the work.
4. Plays defense to survive.	4. Plays offense to make progress.
5. Reacts to needs that arise from moment to moment.	5. Creates opportunities to mentor others.
6. Focuses on immediate needs.	6. Focuses on long-term vision.
7. Shepherds others.	7. Equips others.

Why Pastor-Leaders Fail to Develop People

1. They realize that equipping people is hard work.

2. They are insecure or have a poor self-image.

3. They feel they are the only one qualified to do it.

4. They don't trust others.

5. They have bad habits and an unbiblical perspective.

6. They have a low level of belief in people.

7. They don't know how to train others.

8. It is easier to lead followers than leaders.

Developing others will take energy, time, and careful planning. It is a proactive way of leading, rather than the reactive way many leaders unfortunately run their organizations. It will also mean that, as a leader, you will need to allow others to share ownership of the work you are doing. This requires a belief and trust in others and the ability to relinquish control. However, if you commit to equipping people, you will find Jethro's promise to be true in your life and leadership.

Question: Do you find it difficult to equip other people and delegate tasks? Why?

_____

_____

_____

_____

Question: In what areas could you release control and equip someone to lead?

_____

_____

_____

_____

EXAMINE THE WORD

How Do We Select People to Whom We Can Delegate Work?

This is an important question. Whom do we choose to equip? The answer may be found in Acts 6:1–4 NKJV.

> *Now in those days, when the number of the disciples was multiplying, there arose a complaint against the Hebrews by the Hellenists, because their widows were neglected in the daily distribution. Then the twelve summoned the multitude of the disciples and said, "It is not desirable that we should leave the word of God and serve tables. Therefore, brethren, seek out from among you seven men of good reputation, full of the Holy Spirit and wisdom, whom we may appoint over this business; but we will give ourselves continually to prayer and to the ministry of the word."*

Good leadership responds effectively to the need for more leaders and workers. In the early church, no one took a vote to determine the identity of these people. The apostles had specific qualifications in mind for the leaders they wanted; they chose men who were . . .

1. **Known from their sphere of influence:** *seek out from among you.*

2. **Fellow believers:** *brothers.*

3. **People who could serve on a team:** *seven men.*

4. **Trusted among the people:** *of good reputation.*

5. **Empowered for the task:** *full of the Holy Spirit.*

6. **Competent and intelligent:** *full of . . . wisdom.*

7. **Responsible:** *whom we may appoint over this business.*

How Do We Develop Others While We Delegate the Ministry?

KEY POINTS

1. **Know yourself:** Be familiar with the strengths you pass on to others in the work.

2. **Know the person you wish to develop:** Identify his or her strengths and weaknesses.

3. **Clearly define the assignments:** Don't leave anything in question; write it down.

4. **Teach the "why" behind the assignment:** Let them know why it is important.

5. **Discuss their growth process as you go:** Talk about how they will grow from it.

6. **Spend relational time with them:** Invest time when you are not talking about weaknesses.

7. **Allow them to watch you minister:** Let them observe and get feedback from you.

8. **Give them the resources and authority they need:** Provide the tools to do the job.

9. **Encourage them to journal during the process:** Help them interpret their growth.

10. **Hold them accountable for their ministry:** Get permission to keep them in line.

11. **Give them the freedom to fail:** Communicate that they can learn as they go.

12. **Debrief and affirm regularly:** Encourage them all along the way as they succeed.

What Would Jesus Do?

Then He called His twelve disciples together and gave them power and authority over all demons, and to cure diseases. He sent them to preach the kingdom of God and to heal the sick. (Luke 9:1–2 NKJV)

We see in this passage that Jesus shared both responsibility and authority. To succeed in our missions, we must share both our work and power with a team. Jesus aimed to develop the disciples as He shared the work. He did not spend the majority of His time with the masses. He focused on training the disciples. By not spending equal time with everyone, but more time with those who were ready to be trained, Jesus was able to multiply His ministry in about three years.

The Development Process

1. I do it while you watch.

2. We do it together.

3. You do it while I watch.

4. We evaluate.

5. You do it while another watches.

The Truth about Developing People

Nearly every lasting movement in history endured because the first group of leaders reproduced their leadership and values into a second generation of leaders. It became a movement because it was about multiplication, not addition.

ADDITION LOOKS LIKE THIS: 1 + 1 = 2

MULTIPLICATION LOOKS LIKE THIS:

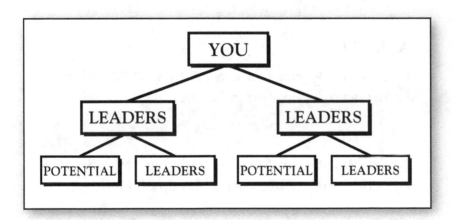

TRUTH IN A PICTURE

Developing Others While Delegating Work

There are several distinctions between a leader of leaders and a leader of followers.

1. DESIRE

Leaders who develop followers . . . NEED TO BE NEEDED. Leaders who develop leaders . . . WANT TO BE SUCCEEDED.

117

2. FOCUS

Leaders who develop followers . . . focus on the WEAKNESSES of people. Leaders who develop leaders . . . focus on the STRENGTHS of people.

3. PRIORITIES

Leaders who develop followers . . . devote effort to those with the most NEEDS. Leaders who develop leaders . . . devote effort to those with the most POTENTIAL.

4. ABILITIES

Leaders who develop followers . . . are GOOD leaders. Leaders who develop leaders . . . are GREAT leaders.

5. ATTITUDE

Leaders who develop followers . . . lift up THEMSELVES. Leaders who develop leaders . . . lift up OTHERS.

6. TIME

Leaders who develop followers . . . SPEND time with people. Leaders who develop leaders . . . INVEST time in people.

7. EXPECTATIONS

Leaders who develop followers . . . ask for LITTLE commitment. Leaders who develop leaders . . . ask for MUCH commitment.

8. LEADERSHIP

Leaders who develop followers . . . lead everyone the SAME. Leaders who develop leaders . . . lead everyone DIFFERENTLY.

9. IMPACT

Leaders who develop followers . . . impact THIS generation. Leaders who develop leaders . . . impact THE NEXT generation.

ASSESSMENT: Am I spending my time developing followers or leaders? How am I cultivating a leadership environment?

ACTION PLAN

APPLICATION: Whom am I developing at this time? Whom can I begin to develop? What is my plan for that person?

_____

_____

_____

_____

Some leaders want to make followers. I want to make leaders.
Not only do I want to make leaders, but leaders of leaders.
And then, leaders of leaders of leaders.
— Dale Galloway

Teamwork Makes the Dream Work

Lesson 10

The Characteristics of a Great Team

BIBLICAL
BASIS

Now there are varieties of gifts, but the same Spirit. And there are varieties of ministries, and the same Lord . . . For even as the body is one and yet has many members, and all the members of the body, though they are many, are one body, so also is Christ. (1 Cor. 12:4–5, 12 NASB)

**KEY
POINTS**

Great Teams Possess:

1. A COMMON GOAL (VISION)

2. DIVERSE SKILLS and CONTRIBUTION

3. STRONG COACHING and COMMUNICATION

What Makes an Effective Team?

1. An effective team CARES FOR ONE ANOTHER.

The foundation of a successful team is relationship. Why?

a. **THE SECOND MILE PRINCIPLE:** People go the "first mile" because of a sense of duty. They go the "second mile" because of relationship.

b. **THE CONNECTION PRINCIPLE:** Leaders always touch a heart before they ask for a hand.

c. **THE HOST PRINCIPLE:** Good leaders always "host" the conversation and relationships of their life. They initiate as a host rather than wait for others to serve, as a guest.

Evaluation: As a team, do we care for one another?

_____

_____

_____

2. An effective team KNOWS and PRACTICES WHAT IS IMPORTANT.

What are your "team's" top three priorities?

a.

b.

c.

Evaluation: As a team, do we know and act on what is important?

_____

_____

_____

3. An effective team GROWS TOGETHER.

Why is growing together, as a staff, so important?

  a. The LEADER'S growth determines the organization's growth.

  b. Life and society are constantly CHANGING.

  c. A leader cannot lead a follower BEYOND where he or she has personally grown.

  d. The leadership team must stay on the "SAME PAGE".

  e. Leaders must IMPROVE to stay in front.

Evaluation: As a team, are we growing together?

4. An effective team HAS A CHEMISTRY THAT FITS.

The right "chemistry" happens on a team when . . .

  a. RELATIONSHIPS are strong.

  b. DESIRES are similar.

  c. TRUST is evident.

  d. ROLES are clear.

  e. ABILITIES are complementary.

  f. PLAYERS are appreciated.

  g. MORALE is high.

  h. WINS are frequent.

  i. MOTIVES are pure.

  j. BENEFITS are received by all.

Evaluation: As a team, do we have the right chemistry?

_____

_____

_____

5. **An effective team PLACES INDIVIDUAL RIGHTS BELOW THE TEAM'S BEST INTEREST.**

The truth in a nutshell: Individualism wins trophies, but teamwork wins championships.

A Code of Cooperation:

a. Carry your load.

b. Respect other team members.

c. Understand teammates' value.

d. Look for ways to add value to teammates.

e. Come together ready to contribute.

f. See the big picture.

g. Give up your rights.

h. Represent the team's position, not yours

i. Privately and publicly affirm one another.

j. Accept responsibility for the team's standings.

Evaluation: As a team, do we place the team's interest above our own?

_____

_____

_____

6. An effective team REALIZES EVERYONE PLAYS A SPECIAL ROLE.

The "Niche Principle": People who occupy a special place on the team feel special and perform in a special way. Team niches humanize teamwork. (Philip VanAuken)

In the margin, list your team members and identify their roles.

What is your unique role on the team?

Evaluation: As a team, do we understand and appreciate the roles of others?

7. An effective team HAS A STRONG BENCH.

In ministry, the bench represents . . .

a. Support players

b. Special role players

c. A place for strategy

d. A place for rest

e. A place for encouragement

f. A place for assistance

8. An effective team KNOWS EXACTLY WHERE THE TEAM STANDS.

The team knows where it stands because there is a scoreboard that everyone can see. Players glance at the scoreboard continually during a game. When the game is over, at least they know if they have won or lost. (Many ministries don't enjoy this luxury!)

127

What areas should be on "our scoreboard"? (i.e. conversions, giving, etc.)

a. _____   c. _____

b. _____   d. _____

9. An effective team PAYS THE PRICE.

There is no success without sacrifice. If I succeed without sacrifice, then it is because someone who went before me made the sacrifice. If I sacrifice and do not see success, then someone who follows will reap success from my sacrifice.

In the margin, list the blessings we have received that we did not pay for.

What sacrifice will we give so that the next generation will have success?

Evaluation: As a team, is our sacrifice sufficient to provide success to the next generation?

_____

_____

_____

10. An effective team SAYS "YES" TO THE RIGHT QUESTIONS.

Ten Questions the Team Should Ask

CHECK
YOUR
HEART

1. Do we RESPECT and TRUST each other? Respect and trust go hand in hand.

2. Do we have CONCERN for each other? Are you honestly interested in the welfare of your colleagues?

3. Do team members feel free to COMMUNICATE openly? In an environment of open and free communication, a team can achieve anything.

4. Do we UNDERSTAND our team's goals? Without a clear focus on team goals, even the best teams will drift.

5. Do we have a COMMITMENT to those goals? Belief in goals should be concrete, not abstract.

6. Do we make good use of each member's ABILITIES? Do members feel they are making a worthwhile contribution?

7. Do we handle CONFLICT successfully? Success is judged by how conflict is handled within the team as a whole.

8. Does EVERYONE participate? The very word "team" implies that everyone participates.

9. Do we respect our individual DIFFERENCES? Do you respect team members with whom you are not always in agreement?

10. Do we LIKE being members of this team? True success depends on enjoying what you do — and that includes enjoying your team.

ACTION PLAN

So Where Do I Begin?

The kinds of people you recruit should be determined by the goals you believe God has given you. Look for appropriate gifts in people for each position.

G — Gifted Members

Look for specific gifts and abilities in other people that are crucial to achieve your goals.

I — Influential People

Look for people who have influence with others.

F — Faithful Workers

Look for people who are already faithful to Christian commitments they have made.

T — Teachable Spirit

Look for people who are willing to learn and be flexible with teammates.

S — Servant's Heart

Look for people who want to serve others, not gain recognition.

Take an Evaluation of Teamwork:

	No	Somewhat	Yes

1. An effective team cares for one another. 1 2 3 4 5

2. An effective team knows what is important. 1 2 3 4 5

3. An effective team grows together. 1 2 3 4 5

4. An effective team has a "team fit." 1 2 3 4 5

5. An effective team places individual rights below the team's best interest. 1 2 3 4 5

6. An effective team realizes that everyone plays a special role. 1 2 3 4 5

7. An effective team has a strong bench. 1 2 3 4 5

8. An effective team knows exactly where it stands. 1 2 3 4 5

9. An effective team pays the price. 1 2 3 4 5

10. An effective team says "yes" to the right questions. 1 2 3 4 5

The Wisest Investment You'll Ever Make

Lesson 11

Mentoring Future Leaders

Then He appointed twelve, that they might be with Him and that He might send them out to preach.
(Mark 3:14 NKJV)

Jesus welcomed people to come to Him for mentoring. He was and is the ultimate mentor. He developed imperfect humans to become effective leaders. Jesus did everything a mentor can do to enable the disciples to flourish in their personal lives and ministry.

In Matthew 11:28–30 NKJV, He says, "Take My yoke upon you, and learn from Me, for I am gentle and lowly in heart, and you will find rest for your souls. For My yoke is easy and My burden is light." In those days a yoke was used for oxen as they labored in the field. The yoke He spoke of was designed to harness two oxen: a strong one and a weak one. The weaker of the two was present to learn what it meant to work in the field through "on the-job" training from the stronger ox. Most of the weight was carried by the strong one until the development process was complete. What a vivid picture of the mentoring process!

A Definition of Mentoring:

A RELATIONAL EXPERIENCE WHERE ONE PERSON EMPOWERS ANOTHER BY SHARING GOD-GIVEN RESOURCES

A Definition of Empowerment:

THE ACT OF GIVING YOUR POWER TO ANOTHER, SO THEY CAN SERVE EFFECTIVELY

Leadership and Commitment

1. We must be committed to a PERSON.

Our mentees must sense our commitment to them as people, not as projects. We must love them and have their best interests in mind. Leaders cannot be developed in massive crowds. They are developed individually through life-on-life mentoring.

Question: Who is someone you could mentor or equip for ministry?

_____

_____

_____

_____

_____

2. We must be committed to a PROCESS.

There will be ups and downs through the season you meet with your mentees. You must step back and see the process they are in and the steps they require for growth, understanding the big picture of their life. We must be discerning.

Question: What steps should you take to train them?

_____

_____

_____

_____

3. We must be committed to a PURPOSE.

Our final commitment must be to the end result. We must determine that we will help them get from where they are to the goal that has been mutually set. Just as God will complete the work He has begun in us (Phil. 1:6), we must see the finished product inside our mentees and fulfill our commitment to them. We must be diligent.

Question: What purpose are you accomplishing?

_____

_____

_____

_____

EXAMINE
THE
WORD

John 15:15 NKJV

No longer do I call you servants, for a servant does not know what his master is doing; but I have called you friends, for all things that I heard from My Father I have made known to you.

Matthew 28:18–20 NKJV

And Jesus came and spoke to them, saying, "All authority has been given to Me in heaven and on earth. Go therefore and make disciples of all the nations, baptizing them in the name of the Father and of the Son and of the Holy Spirit, teaching them to observe all things that I have commanded you; and lo, I am with you always, even to the end of the age." Amen.

The Process of Training Leaders

STEP 1: Model

The process begins with the mentor doing the tasks while the mentee watches. Be sure to give the mentee the opportunity to see the whole process. Too often the mentor begins in the middle of the task and confuses the mentee. When the mentee sees the task performed correctly and completely, it demonstrates the process to imitate.

STEP 2: Mentor

During this next step, the mentor will continue to perform the task, but this time the mentee comes alongside and assists in the process. Take time to explain not only the *how* but also the *why* of each step. There should be lots of communication happening at this stage.

Lesson 11: The Wisest Investment You'll Ever Make

STEP 3: Monitor

At this point, the mentor and the mentee exchange places. The mentee performs the task and the mentor will assist and correct. It is especially important during this phase to be positive and encouraging to the mentee. It will help the mentee to keep on trying and wanting to improve rather than give up. Work together to develop consistency. Once the mentee understands the process, have him/her explain it back to the mentor. The explanation will reinforce the process in the mentee's memory.

STEP 4: Motivate

At this point the mentor will step out of the task and relinquish the responsibility to the mentee. The assignment of the mentor is to make sure the mentee has the knowledge to do the task and the encouragement to continue to improve. It is important for the mentor to stay with the mentee until success is realized. This will motivate the mentee to make improvements to the process.

STEP 5: Multiply

Once the mentee does the job well, the next step is for the mentee to become a mentor. As teachers know, the best way to learn something is to teach it. The beauty of the mentoring process is that it allows the mentor to move on to other important developmental tasks while the new leader is now capable of fulfilling various tasks and leading others.

TRUTH IN A PICTURE

A candle loses nothing when it lights another; instead it doubles its brightness. This is how mentoring works. Leaders invest their time and insight into an emerging leader and begin to multiply their effort. While the work seems slow at first, it grows at an exponential rate!

Gifts that Good Mentors Give Away

KEY POINTS

1. THEY PAINT PICTURES.

The human mind thinks in pictures. We are visual people living in a visual age. Stories, analogies and metaphors help us to retain important information. When mentors paint pictures with their words, it helps those being mentored to grasp the concepts they are being taught. Mentors paint pictures through stories, analogies, word pictures, and parables.

2. THEY PROVIDE HANDLES.

Everyone possesses some knowledge of truth. Most people, however, are determined to understand it so strongly that they can use it in everyday life. Simply put, "handles" are things we can grab on to. We give people handles when we summarize truths into a "user friendly" fashion. The truth then becomes a principle they can live by. When someone has a handle on something, it means they own it and can practice it, as well as communicate it to others. A good mentor can distill or *crystallize* truth so that the complex becomes simple.

3. THEY OFFER ROAD MAPS.

Road maps are items that help give us both direction and a big-picture view. When we give someone a road map we are passing on a life compass to them. That map helps us travel on roads we've never known. These spiritual road maps help people not only see the right road, but also see its relation to all other roads. They provide perspective on the whole picture. This generally happens only when we communicate intentionally, not accidentally.

4. THEY SUPPLY LABORATORIES.

When we provide laboratories for our mentees, we are giving them a place to practice the truth we've discussed with them. By definition, laboratories are safe places in which to experiment. We all need a lab to accompany all the knowledge and teaching we receive. In these labs, we learn the right questions to ask, the appropriate exercises to practice, an understanding of the issues, and experiential knowledge of what our agenda should be in life. Good laboratories are measurable and can be evaluated together.

5. THEY FURNISH ROOTS.

One of the most crucial goals a mentor ought to have for their mentee is to give them roots and wings. This popular phrase describes everyone's need for foundations to be laid, as well as the freedom to soar and to broaden their horizons. The foundation we must help to lay in our mentee involves the construction of a *character-based* life versus an *emotion-based* life. At the end of their time together, the mentee should possess strong convictions they

139

can live by, as well as the self-esteem to stand behind those convictions. The deeper the roots, the taller the tree can grow, and the more durable that tree is during the storm.

6. THEY GIVE WINGS.

The final word picture that describes what a mentor provides for a mentee is wings. We give others wings when we enable them to think big, and expect big things from God and themselves. When people possess wings, they are free to explore and to plumb the depths of their own potential. When mentors give wings, they help mentees to soar to new heights in their lives. Consequently, it's as important to teach those mentees how to ask the questions as much as how to obtain the answers.

Question: Which of these "gifts" do you give away to others?

_____

_____

_____

EXAMINE THE WORD

Jesus's Example of Mentoring

Jesus faced the task of changing the lives of people thousands of years after Him — and He succeeded. He did it without writing any books, building any schools, or founding any institutions. So if Jesus chose to deposit His legacy in people, we should learn His method and practice it as best as we can. In the Bible, we find the ideal model of a mentor to follow in Jesus, the Master-Teacher. The following is how He did it . . .

1. **INSTRUCTION in a life-related context:** He taught and instructed them verbally.

   Jesus constantly taught, most often with parables, and discussed hundreds of issues with the twelve. When the disciples would ask Him the meaning of a parable, He explained it, revealing insightful truth wrapped in a story. While His mentoring was so much more than "words," it did, indeed, involve careful instructions on His part.

   . . . Jesus went up the mountainside with his disciples and sat down to teach them . . . (Matthew 5:1 NLT)

2. **DEMONSTRATION in a life-related context:** He modeled truths for the disciples to observe.

   Educational philosophy today relies too heavily on instruction. If Jesus had simply taught the disciples and had done nothing more, they never would have carried on His legacy. But Jesus shared His life with them. He deliberately gave the disciples His life as an example to watch. He knew they would learn faster if He showed them, not just told them. He taught with His life.

   For I have given you an example, that you should do as I have done to you. (John 13:15 NKJV)

3. **EXPERIENCE in a life-related context:** He let the disciples participate and apply truth themselves.

   After Jesus had modeled good leadership and taught spiritual truths, He didn't turn His men loose and move on. He gradually worked them into positions of independent leadership by giving them valuable experience. Jesus transferred the responsibility He felt for advancing God's kingdom to His mentees (disciples). Jesus gave His followers an opportunity to practice what He had taught and to practice leadership. He gave them all ownership for the ministry through delegation and authority.

And He called the twelve to Himself, and began to send them out two by two, and gave them power over unclean spirits. (Mark 6:7 NKJV)

4. **ASSESSMENT in a life-related context:** He debriefed their shared experience and assessed their growth.

Jesus repeatedly evaluated the progress of His disciples. After the return of the seventy, He debriefed them, gave them instruction concerning priorities, and celebrated with them (Luke 10:17–24). He also gave individual assessment to His disciples, including specific feedback concerning their character and their capabilities. Once He trusted them with tasks, He knew they would need accountability on their performance.

Nevertheless do not rejoice in this, that the spirits are subject to you, but rather rejoice because your names are written in heaven. (Luke 10:20 NKJV)

The beautiful part about these principles is that every one of us can apply them. They are transferable concepts that anyone — in any generation, in any location — can practice. If you want to leave a legacy, you must look for people to carry it for you. Find the right people and use the right preparation process for each of them. Only as you pour yourself into them will they be able to pour themselves out for others. No one can give what he does not have.

How to Get Started

ACTION PLAN

a. Pray for God to help you own the vision for mentoring other leaders.

b. Select a potential mentee or group of mentees from your circle of influence.

c. Spend two initial meetings to discuss both of your expectations and goals.

d. Cast vision to them for spiritual reproduction and leadership multiplication.

e. Determine what tool or resource you will study together.

f. Ask for commitment.

g. Determine how long and how often you will meet.

h. Be prepared and set goals.

i. Discuss and apply the truths together.

j. Evaluate their progress regularly.

k. Help them find potential leaders to mentor.

l. Pray for the Holy Spirit's anointing and launch them to multiply!

Remember, the mentoring process will feel slow at first. It is all about a movement, not a program. Programs usually start very big, then eventually lose momentum and become very small. Movements are just the opposite. They usually start very small, and grow very large.

The Son of God selected twelve men, not twelve hundred men. He said the Kingdom grows like a mustard seed. It is the smallest of seeds in the beginning, but eventually grows so large that birds can build nests in its branches. We are about a movement as we train leaders.

When You Meet, Offer Them these Resources

Even if you've never really mentored other leaders before, you have the ability to offer some resources to them immediately. The following eight resources are ones that don't require you to learn a single new truth in order to provide them for a potential leader. Why not begin offering them to a small cluster of emerging leaders as you find them?

1. **ACCOUNTABILITY:** Ask tough questions; help them keep commitments.

2. **AFFIRMATION:** Offer words of encouragement and support; affirm their strengths.

3. **ASSESSMENT:** Evaluate their condition objectively; help them gain perspective.

4. **ACCEPTANCE:** Provide unconditional love and grace to them even when they fail.

5. **ADVICE:** Speak words of wise counsel and give them options for their decisions.

6. **ADMONITION:** Offer words of caution and warning so they can avoid pitfalls.

7. **ASSETS:** Give them tangible gifts and resources — a book, a tape, or a personal contact.

8. **APPLICATION:** Direct them to discover how they can practice what they've learned.

EMPOWERING PEOPLE		
SHEPHERDING BELIEVERS	EQUIPPING WORKERS	DEVELOPING LEADERS
Care	Training for ministry	Training for personal growth
Immediate-need focus	Task-focus	Person-focus
Relational	Transactional	Transformational
Service	Management	Leadership
Ministry by maintenance	Ministry by addition	Ministry by multiplication
Immediate	Short term	Long term
Feeling better	Unleashing	Empowering
Availability	Teaching	Mentoring
Focus on nurture	Focus on specific ministry	Focus on specific leader
No curriculum	Set curriculum	Flexible curriculum
Need-oriented	Skill-oriented	Character-oriented
Maintenance	Doing	Being
What is the problem?	What do I need?	What do they need?
Problem-focused	Purpose-focused	Person-focused
They begin to walk	They'll walk the first mile	They'll walk the second mile

ACTION PLAN

ASSESSMENT: Who are some people you could mentor and develop?

_____

_____

_____

_____

_____

APPLICATION: When will you begin the process?

_____

_____

_____

_____

_____

We must commit ourselves to reproduce and multiply.

Measuring Your Leadership Growth

Lesson 12

An Evaluation for Growing Leaders

BIBLICAL BASIS

Search me, O God, and know my heart; Test me and know my anxious thoughts. See if there is any offensive way in me, and lead me in the way everlasting. (Ps. 139:23–24 NIV)

In this chapter, let's push the pause button and evaluate your leadership growth. Take time to stop now and measure the central qualities that healthy, effective, lasting leaders possess. This list of characteristics is timeless and universal. It will measure your leadership qualities. Talk about your responses to these with the rest of the group. Do others agree with your assessment? Let's get started.

1. CHARACTER

Strong character enables leaders to possess integrity, to earn trust, to gain respect, to experience consistency, and to communicate credibility.

Contagious Leadership Workbook

KEY POINTS

Character is the sum-total of four ingredients in a leader's life:

a. **PERSONAL IDENTITY:** A strong moral compass only comes through people who have established their identities as "new creatures in Christ." They don't have to prove anything or hide anything. This breeds trust among others.

b. **EMOTIONAL SECURITY:** God desires to construct in us a positive mental and emotional framework. Emotional stability is like the infrastructure that holds a leader up in crisis.

c. **ETHICS AND VALUES:** Leaders must be principle-centered. They can't drift with the culture and change the foundation on which they stand morally or spiritually. Values include the ethics and principles for which we stand and on which we stand.

d. **SELF-DISCIPLINE:** We must determine that we will lead our own lives well before we can expect anyone else to follow us. As Paul says in 1 Timothy 3:5 NIV, "If anyone does not know how to manage his own family, how can he take care of God's church?"

CHECK YOUR HEART

As you think about your own character, rate yourself on the following:

a. I assume responsibility for myself and my team.

1   2   3   4   5   6   7   8   9   10

b. I am secure in my identity and my self-esteem.

1   2   3   4   5   6   7   8   9   10

c. I do what I should, even when I don't feel like it.

1   2   3   4   5   6   7   8   9   10

Character is the foundation upon which we build our leadership. When we have this foundation in place, we can move on to building other necessary qualities.

2. COMPASSION

While the issue of character deals with the world's perception of a leader, compassion deals with the leader's perception of others in the world. Compassion is a virtue that takes seriously the reality of other persons, their inner lives, their emotions, as well as their external circumstances.

How well do you express compassion for others? Does compassion move you to meet the needs of others and help solve problems? Respond to these statements:

a. I will help those in need even when it costs me.

1   2   3   4   5   6   7   8   9   10

b. I am moved emotionally by my love for others.

1   2   3   4   5   6   7   8   9   10

c. I am fulfilled when I serve and meet others' needs.

1   2   3   4   5   6   7   8   9   10

3. COURAGE

Once character has been developed to include compassion for others, it takes courage to implement change. Having courage means facing fears and taking stands. It means acting brave when we don't really feel brave.

How well do you exhibit courage? Take a moment and evaluate yourself.

a. I like to start new projects, even when it's scary.

1   2   3   4   5   6   7   8   9   10

b. I don't mind being the first to take a risk.

1   2   3   4   5   6   7   8   9   10

c. When ideas arise, I want to take action, not talk.

1   2   3   4   5   6   7   8   9   10

4. COMPETENCY

A leader of character must be capable of convincing followers that he or she is competent enough to get the job done. A competent leader has the ingenuity and creativity to figure out what to do and how to do it.

Have you stopped to evaluate your level of competency? What abilities do you bring to the table?

a. My ideas often turn into plans.

1   2   3   4   5   6   7   8   9   10

b. I can figure out how to finish a job I start.

   1   2   3   4   5   6   7   8   9   10

c. I am good at solving problems.

   1   2   3   4   5   6   7   8   9   10

5. CONVICTIONS

A conviction is a strong belief that so governs your decisions that you are willing to die for it. Convictions usually revolve around the values a leader embraces. The following seven action steps will help you build convictions into your life:

a. Summarize and MEDITATE on major principles from God's Word.

b. Repeatedly expose yourself to NEEDS around you.

c. Interview people who possess deep CONVICTIONS.

d. Determine your LIFE MISSION and values.

e. Make an all-out COMMITMENT to a habit for a set time.

f. Learn the WHYs behind the Scripture.

g. Get someone to hold you ACCOUNTABLE to your convictions.

Consider the strength of your convictions:

a. I know exactly what I believe.

   1   2   3   4   5   6   7   8   9   10

153

b. I make sacrifices because of my beliefs.

1   2   3   4   5   6   7   8   9   10

c. Passion enables me to act on what I believe.

1   2   3   4   5   6   7   8   9   10

6. COMMITMENT

Conviction goes hand-in-hand with another important principle — commitment. Commitment is needed most when a leader encounters routine obstacles or unsettling failures.

Are you committed to anything, as a leader? Consider these statements.

a. I finish what I start.

1   2   3   4   5   6   7   8   9   10

b. Obstacles don't discourage me but challenge me.

1   2   3   4   5   6   7   8   9   10

c. I can stay focused on one goal.

1   2   3   4   5   6   7   8   9   10

7. CHARISMA

Charisma enables leaders to accomplish more. This topic, mystical to many, is often misunderstood. Plainly stated, charisma is the ability to draw people to you — being a magnet for others.

a. **LOVE life:** The people you enjoy being around are celebrators, not complainers.

b. **Expect the BEST of others:** Encourage others to reach their potential.

c. **Give people HOPE:** People are grateful when they are given the gift of hope.

d. **SHARE yourself:** People love leaders who are transparent.

When it comes to charisma, the bottom line is other-mindedness. Leaders who think about others and their concerns before thinking of themselves exhibit charisma. This is the one quality that will draw others to you more than anything else.

What do you possess that attracts others to you or helps you connect with them? Think about your response to these statements. Do they describe you?

a. When I enter a room, I think of others, not myself.

1   2   3   4   5   6   7   8   9   10

b. I give confidence and encouragement to others.

1   2   3   4   5   6   7   8   9   10

c. I am genuinely interested in other people.

1   2   3   4   5   6   7   8   9   10

SUMMARY

It's important to view these qualities as acquired characteristics that need to be developed, rather than assuming they are personality traits that cannot be acquired. All seven are crucial

Contagious Leadership Workbook

to learning leadership and even more crucial to mentoring others to be leaders.

ACTION PLAN

ASSESSMENT: Review your evaluations. Out of these seven qualities, which are your strongest?

_____

_____

_____

_____

APPLICATION: On which do you need to work?

_____

_____

_____

_____

About the Authors

Dr. John Hull
President/CEO, EQUIP.

A frequent speaker at local churches and global outreach events, Hull regularly provides leadership training to audiences in Asia, Europe, the Middle East and Far East, Africa, and the Americas.

Prior to his work with EQUIP, Hull served congregations in the United States and Canada, most recently as Senior Pastor of Peoples Church in Toronto. He earned a degree in journalism and telecommunications from the University of Georgia, a Master of Divinity degree from Liberty Baptist Theological Seminary, and a Doctor of Ministry degree from Gordon-Conwell Theological Seminary.

EQUIP's founder, John Maxwell, says: "John Hull's vast relationships in the evangelical world add tremendous value to EQUIP's on-going mission of training leaders worldwide. He's without question a valued member of my inner circle."

Hull monthly hosts *"The Global Stage,"* where he interviews leaders from around the world who assist EQUIP in training and resourcing hundreds of thousands of leaders worldwide. *Leadership Moment*, a radio ministry of EQUIP, is also hosted by Hull as well as the EQUIP *President's Forum*, which provides mentoring forums for emerging pastors across the United States twice a year.

Hull has written numerous magazine articles and co-authored *Pivotal Praying* with Tim Elmore. He also writes a bi-monthly column on leadership and global concerns for Christianworkplace.com. John resides in Atlanta with his wife Sharon, and two children, Andy and Mary Alice.

Dr. Doug Carter
Senior Vice President, EQUIP.

Doug Carter has served as Senior Vice President at EQUIP. since 1996. Previously, Doug and his wife, Winnie, served as missionaries to Native Americans for more than sixteen years. In 1980, Dr. Carter became president of Circleville Bible College where he served nine years, helping prepare men and women for Christian service.

From 1989 until he joined EQUIP. in 1996, Carter served as Vice President of World Gospel Mission, an interdenominational mission agency with 330 career missionaries sharing the gospel in twenty-four nations. He is an outstanding communicator who has ministered in more than eighty nations worldwide.

Carter is the author of *Big Picture People*, published by Beacon Hill Press. His book is a vital resource for Christians who want to press beyond mediocrity and rise to excellence in their faith. He has also written booklets about ministry funding, partnership, and biblical stewardship.

Carter represents EQUIP. in churches and conferences across America and teaches in EQUIP. leadership conferences around the world. He also serves on the boards of several other Christian organizations. Doug and Winnie reside in Atlanta. They are the parents of three children—Angie, Eric and Jason.

Dr. Tim Elmore
Vice President of Leadership Development, EQUIP.

Serving as Vice President of Leadership Development at EQUIP., Tim has ministered in thirty-four countries, including India, Russia, China, England, Egypt, Lebanon, Australia, Argentina, several countries in Europe, and the Philippines. He is committed to developing young leaders and pastors on every continent of the world.

Since 1983, Tim has served under and been mentored by Dr. John Maxwell. He has served as a pastor at two churches and vice president of two organizations since 1979. He received his Bachelor's degree from Oral Roberts University and his Master of Divinity and Doctor of Ministry degrees from Azusa Pacific University.

Tim is the Founder and president of "Growing Leaders," a non-profit organization created to develop emerging leaders. Through Growing Leaders, he and his team are equipping middle school, high school, and college students on hundreds of campuses in the U.S. including Duke, Rutgers, Florida State, and in Christian colleges such as Biola University, Bethel College, Asbury College, and Regent University. This is his passion, having worked with students since 1979. In addition, Tim has equipped leaders in corporations such as Chick-fil-A, HomeBanc, Gold Kist, and Home and Garden Party.

Tim has authored numerous books, including the bestselling series *Habitudes: Images That Form Leadership Habits and Attitudes*. Tim is the author of *Nurturing the Leader Within Your Child*, *Soul Provider*, *Authentic Influence*, *Wired for Influence*, *Intentional Influence*, and *Leveraging Your Influence*, and is the co-author of *Pivotal Praying*. In addition to

163

leadership, Tim has a passion for mentoring and practices this ministry with leaders each year at his church. He has written *Mentoring: How to Invest Your Life in Others* and *The Greatest Mentors in the Bible* which communicate this passion.

Tim lives in Atlanta with his wife Pam and his two children, Bethany and Jonathan.

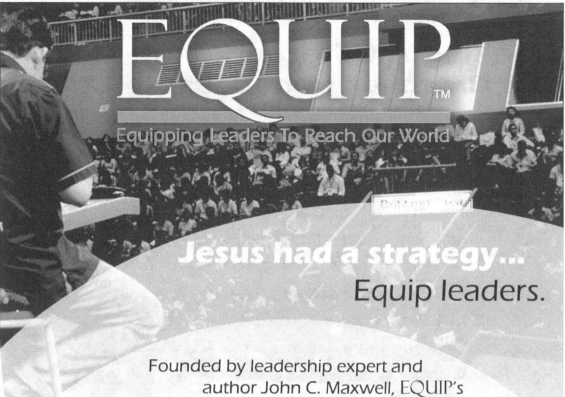

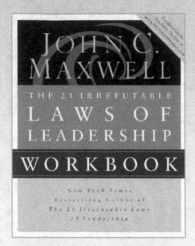

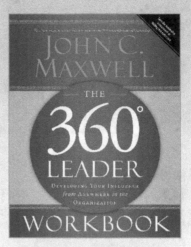

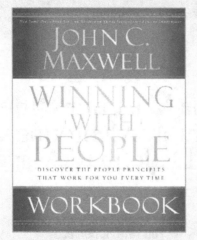

Continue developing your own essential leadership skills with one of these great workbooks from one of the world's most recognized leadership experts—John Maxwell.

THE LEADERSHIP EXPERT, JOHN C. MAXWELL, TAKES AN IN-DEPTH LOOK AT GOD'S LAWS FOR LEADERS AND LEADERSHIP.

The people, events, and teachings of the Bible are a treasury of wisdom and guidance for anyone who has been called to be a leader, to develop leaders, or to work with leaders—in church, business, commerce, or anyplace else. The Maxwell Leadership Bible shows us what God's Word has to say to people of all kinds about leaders and leadership. It's a Bible resource that explains book by book what a godly leader is, what leadership means, what empowering others is about, and how God is glorified when we're all involved in His leadership plan for us.

FEATURES INCLUDE:

- THE 21 LAWS OF LEADERSHIP: A BIBLICAL PERSPECTIVE Biblical people who exemplified each of the 21 Laws of Leadership

- THE 21 QUALITIES OF A LEADER Profiles good and bad examples of biblical leadership and what it takes to lead

- BOOK INTRODUCTIONS FOR LEADERSHIP Introductions that focus on leadership, God's role in each book, leaders and people of influence, and lessons in leadership

- BIOGRAPHICAL PROFILES The times and events in biblical people's lives that reveal the most about God's truths of leadership are spotlighted and developed.

- LEADERSHIP ISSUES Hundreds of articles explaining the important events and teachings in the Bible that instruct us about scriptural principles of leadership.

- THOUGHTS FOR LEADERS AND FOLLOWERS Hundreds of concise and expressive notes that illustrate what the Bible has to show us about leadership, mentoring, and influence.

- Subject Indexes

AVAILABLE IN STORES NOW

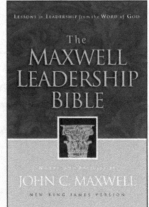

NELSON BIBLES
A Division of Thomas Nelson Publishers
Since 1798

NKJV
NEW KING JAMES VERSION®
Build Your Life On It.™

9 781418 517847